Edward M. Goulburn

The Lord's Prayer

by E. M. Goulburn

Edward M. Goulburn

The Lord's Prayer
by E. M. Goulburn

ISBN/EAN: 9783337276447

Printed in Europe, USA, Canada, Australia, Japan

Cover: Foto ©Lupo / pixelio.de

More available books at **www.hansebooks.com**

THE
LORD'S PRAYER

BY

THE LATE E. M. GOULBURN, D.D.

SOMETIME DEAN OF NORWICH

LONDON

JOHN MURRAY, ALBEMARLE STREET

1898

PREFACE

These meditations on the Lord's Prayer were originally delivered in the form of Sermons. They were frequently made use of, and carefully revised, by the late Dean, for the instruction of various congregations. Possibly intended for publication in something of the same manner as his 'Thoughts on Personal Religion,' they seem to have been kept, in the meantime, by their pious and learned author, as a private store of thought on their great subject.

The editing required for their present form has been chiefly the omission of recapitulations and repetitions necessary in the separate sermons of a series, but not required for a collection in a single book. Two or three notes have been added in explanation and support of the author's arguments.

B. COMPTON.

CONTENTS

CHAP.		PAGE
I.	The Structure and Completeness of the Lord's Prayer	1
II.	The Context of the Lord's Prayer	21
III.	The Sources of the Lord's Prayer	36
IV.	The Two Records of the Lord's Prayer	56
V.	Our Father which art in Heaven	76
VI.	Hallowed be Thy Name	95
VII.	Thy Kingdom Come	115
VIII.	Thy Will be done	137
IX.	As in Heaven, so in Earth	158
X.	Give us this Day our Daily Bread	175
XI.	Our Daily Bread	192
XII.	And Forgive us our Debts	206
XIII.	As we Forgive our Debtors	222
XIV.	And Lead us not into Temptation	240
XV.	But Deliver us from Evil	265
XVI.	For Thine is the Kingdom, and the Power, and the Glory, for ever.—Amen	282

THE LORD'S PRAYER

CHAPTER I

THE STRUCTURE AND COMPLETENESS OF THE LORD'S PRAYER.

Our Father which art in heaven,
    Hallowed be Thy Name:
    Thy Kingdom come:
    Thy Will be done:
In earth, as it is in heaven.
    Give us this day our daily bread:
    And forgive us our debts, as we forgive our debtors:
    And lead us not into temptation:
    But deliver us from evil:
For Thine is the Kingdom, and the Power, and the Glory, for ever. Amen.

THERE are on record three prayers of our Divine Lord, each of which presents Him to us in a different aspect. In one of them, He appears in His human soul, shrinking with all the sensitiveness of innocence from the cruel necessity imposed on Him by the work of human redemption which He had undertaken; 'O My Father, if it be possible, let this cup pass from Me: nevertheless, not as I will, but as Thou wilt.'

In another He appears as a Prophet or Teacher, instructing His disciples after what manner they are to approach God, He Himself not being involved in the prayer which He dictates; for how could He who was 'holy, harmless, undefiled'—who had no trespasses—pray, 'Forgive us our trespasses'?

This is the Lord's Prayer.

In the third prayer, He appears as a Priest interceding for His people; He embraces both Himself and them in His petition, asking for His own glorification and for theirs with Him.

This is the prayer in the seventeenth chapter of St. John, usually called the Great Highpriestly Prayer.

Thus we have from the Lord's lips one prayer for Himself exclusively, one prayer for His

Church exclusively, and one prayer for Himself and His Church together.

As in the Ten Commandments we have a complete and exhaustive summary of all the principles of human duty, the seed of all religious precept; so in the Lord's Prayer do we find the seed of all prayer. Or, to vary slightly the image, we have here under our hands the gamut of prayer, the seven simple notes, in which is latent, and from which may be elicited, the harmony of every prayer which has ever been sounded forth from the human heart in the ear of God.

For the great marvellousness of the Lord's Prayer lies, like the marvellousness of the Decalogue, in its completeness, in the impossibility of adding another petition to it without tautology, and of abstracting a single word without the forfeiture of an idea. Other moralists and legislators besides Moses may have promulgated some one or more of the Ten Commandments. There are found here and there, in the writings of heathen sages, stray, straggling sentiments of a very grand and disinterested morality. But in vain can we seek among the heathen for any code so systematic as the Decalogue, so reaching to the first foundations of the subject, so masterly in its divisions, so thoroughly exhaustive in its treatment.

The case of the Lord's Prayer is very similar. The detached petitions of the Lord's Prayer, and even the invocation, 'Our Father which art in heaven,' may have been separately floating about in the Jewish devotional literature before our Lord compiled and digested them into one perfect form. He created out of these previously existing materials a prayer which has in its absolute completeness the trace of the Divine workmanship, according to that profound word of Solomon's descriptive of God's handiwork: 'I know that whatsoever God doeth, it shall be for ever; *nothing can be put to it, nor anything taken from it.*'

And now, first, as to the grouping of the various parts of this prayer. There are two tables of the law, one teaching us our duty to God, the other our duty to our neighbour. Correspondently we find the body of this prayer falling into two great divisions: (1) petitions for God's glory in the three first clauses, 'Hallowed be Thy name,' 'Thy kingdom come,' 'Thy will be done'; and (2) petitions for the supply of man's necessities in the four last clauses, 'Give us this day our daily bread,' 'Forgive us our trespasses,' 'Lead us not into temptation,' 'Deliver us from evil.' Three and four make seven; and seven is one of the mystical numbers indicating completeness. So it was that on the seventh day God rested, after completing His work of creation, regarding it as 'very good,' i.e. supremely accomplished.

A foundation is laid for the prayer to stand upon by the invocation with which it opens; 'Our Father which art in heaven.' And as the prayer is built upon this foundation, so it is terminated in St. Matthew's Gospel by a beautiful finial in the ascription of praise; 'For Thine is the Kingdom, and the Power, and the Glory, for ever. Amen.'

Prayer comes forth from God, and returns to God. It is the voice of His Spirit in man's heart. And when it has finished its course, it pours itself again, in the shape of adoration, into the bosom of Him from whom it originated.

And this general arrangement of the composition penetrates to the very foundation of the subject. What a clear and beautiful light does it throw on the two great aspects of prayer! As the Decalogue teaches that duty to God is the essential foundation of all duty, so the Lord's Prayer teaches that homage to God, quite independently of the necessities of man, is the fundamental idea of all prayer.

Two totally distinct views may be taken of prayer. The commonest and most superficial view is that the one object of prayer is for the supply of man's wants, as though a man should say, I need some blessing, bodily or spiritual; and I go to the Throne of Grace to petition for it. In this view he is a suitor, nothing more. But the higher and more fundamental view of prayer is that of an exercise, by which man does homage to the Father, and at the same time to his Redeemer, and to the Sanctifier of his spirit. A man must prostrate himself in worship before the Uncreated Light and the

Uncreated Love. In this view he is not a suitor, but a worshipper offering a spiritual sacrifice, acceptable to God by Jesus Christ. And he must do this homage as a worshipper, before he represents his necessities as a suitor.

The practical bearing of this doctrine is that we are not to snatch selfishly and covetously at the blessings which God holds in His Hand, before we have rendered to Him in our hearts that adoration which is His due. Our petitions for self should flow out of, and take their tone from, homage done to our Creator. Get your heart warmed with right and great conceptions of God before you enter upon the business of your suit. Seek to be penetrated with the thought of His wisdom, blessedness, beauty, and love; think that the praise of all the harps of all the angels falls far below His excellence, and that He deserves infinitely more than all the love of every human heart which ever was or ever shall be created. Thus, to take the lowest ground, will thy prayers for self be most successful. The peevish and greedy child who cares not so much for the parent as for what he has to give, may easily fail of his petitions to a wise and good father, however clamorously urged; but few parents can resist large confidence and warm affection displayed towards them by a child. And, similarly, a deep veneration of God's fatherhood, a high regard for His name, for His kingdom, and His will, cannot fail to draw out from Him, and down upon ourselves, if not what we solicit, yet at all events a richer and a better blessing.

In embarking upon the first group of petitions, it should be understood that the clause, 'As it is in heaven,' applies not merely to the last, but to each one of them. We pray that God's name may be hallowed in earth as it is in heaven, and that His kingdom may come in earth as it already is in heaven, no less than that His will may be done upon earth as it is in heaven.

In short, our Blessed Lord, who came down from heaven, points us in thought at the beginning of our prayer to the bright sphere from which He came, and proposes to us angelic worship, angelic service, and angelic obedience as our rightful model. There is something exceedingly refreshing in the survey thus suggested of heavenly love and zeal and order, before we come down to the workday needs, and sins, and trials of this toilsome, troublesome world!

First, *Angelic Worship.* 'Hallowed be Thy name, in earth, &c.' The name of God in the Holy Scriptures stands for God in His revealed attributes and character; and the petition is that God may be venerated and adored by us, as He is in the habitation of His holiness and His glory; or, in the inimitably simple and deep language of our Catechism, that 'All people may worship Him as they ought to do.'

A glimpse is given us by the Prophet Isaiah of the seraphim standing before the throne with veiled faces and feet, and crying one to another, 'Holy, Holy, Holy, is the Lord of Hosts; the whole earth is full of His glory.' We pray that God may be acknowledged as holy in the hearts of men, just as He is by the Seraphim, that the beauty and awfulness of His character may be universally recognized. This is a petition on behalf of God's Person. We begin with His

Personality, before we proceed to any other thoughts connected with Him.

Secondly, *Angelic Service*. 'That all people may serve Him as they ought to do'; 'Thy kingdom come in earth as in heaven.' The holy angels are not engaged in adoration only, but in service also. In the passage just referred to, which is descriptive of angelic homage, we are told, 'Each one had six wings. With twain he covered his face, and with twain he covered his feet' (this is adoration, after the oriental manner of rendering it); but it is added, 'With twain he did fly'—fly to the execution of those ministries with which God charged him. He goes to Nazareth, to announce Messiah's birth to the humble maiden destined to be His mother; or to the wilderness, to minister to the Son of God, when the devil has left Him; or to Gethsemane, to recruit the failing powers of His humanity; or to the Mount of Ascension, to instruct and console bereaved disciples; or to Herod's prison, to liberate St. Peter; or to a ship's cabin on the tossing waves of the Adriatic, to assure St. Paul of the deliverance of himself and his fellow-voyagers. We men have a similar privilege of being instruments of God's service, each of us more or less directly. Our earthly vocations and pursuits are tasks set us by Him, and all contribute something—some more, some less—to the great scheme of His service. That all may work for God in their various positions, and thus forward that glorious kingdom which shall be set up visibly at the second Advent of Christ—this is the substance of the second petition, which is on behalf of God's service, as the first was on behalf of His Person.

Thirdly, *Angelic Obedience.* 'That we may obey Him as we ought to do'; 'Thy will be done in earth, as it is in Heaven.'

Obedience is a distinct thought from Service. Obedience (including resignation) is the prerogative of free will. *All* creatures, even the irrational and inanimate, serve God in their several spheres; for service may be done by constraint, by the operation of a law which it is impossible to escape. But obedience and submission can only be yielded by free agents, such as men and angels. To men (though not to angels) obedience and submission are often hard trials; we often find it difficult to yield them. And therefore here is insinuated for the first time the thought of man's sorrows and sins; so that this petition, like the fifth precept of the Decalogue, acts as a sort of bridge by which we pass from the first to the second part of the Prayer. We pray that we may obey God's commandments and (which involves the same principle) submit to His providential appointments, with the zeal, and cheerfulness, and confidence in His wisdom which the angels exhibit. And with this petition on behalf of God's will we close the first section of our prayer, and proceed to the second. We remove our eyes from the heaven above, on which we have been fixing them, and throw them around us upon earth.

And when we do so, what observations have we to make upon man's condition? If we were required to state in three words the great features of man's condition, as experience makes them known to us, could we name three more characteristic and comprehensive features than these—Want, Sin, Trial? And these features are traced in the Lord's Prayer in the order in which we have experience of them in human life. In a little infant, sin is latent and cannot exhibit itself. But though the infant makes no exhibition of sin, he makes a hundred exhibitions of want. Beyond all creatures on the face of the earth, the human infant is most dependent, most full of wants. But the infant grows to be a child; and then in trickery, in greediness, in selfishness, in temper, the other feature of man's condition is developed. This child is clearly a sinner, before it can yet understand fully the nature and force of temptation, and while we say of it compassionately, 'All its trials are yet to come.' When the child becomes a young man or young woman, it then feels the strength of passion and the attractiveness of the world's lures, which are two chief sources of temptation; and as the young man or young woman grow older, they contract acquaintance with trial in the shape of ill health, or poverty, or bereavement, or anxieties. When you have said this, you have not much more to observe on the outline of man's estate. So the great Prophet and Prayer-giver prescribes first, *A prayer for human wants*; 'Give us this day our daily bread.' Our dependence upon God for the supply of our wants, the daily acknowledgement of this dependence which it becomes us to make, the propriety of asking for simple necessaries, not for luxuries, and generally of being very modest and sparing in our petitions for earthly good, are all indicated here with the utmost brevity and comprehensiveness. But if our Heavenly Father were to supply our bodily necessities, and maintain us in life and health, without at the same time pardoning our sins, the prolongation of life would in fact be only an increase of our condemnation; for every day we should only be adding to the account which stands against us in the debt-book of God's strict justice. Therefore, with a profound significance, the prayer for bread is tied to one for mercy; 'Give us this day our daily bread'; *and* (concurrently with the gift) 'forgive us our trespasses.' At this point it is that we connect the prayer with the great Atonement, whose efficacy alone can procure its acceptance. For who is it that has put these words into our mouths? Who hath taught us thus to pray? Our Lord Jesus, who hath made a full, perfect, and sufficient sacrifice, oblation, and satisfaction for the sins of the whole world. We go to God, when we use this Prayer, in the character of Christ's disciples, and in His Name. And if in His Name, then on the ground of His work of mediation and intercession.

The clause, 'as we forgive them that trespass against us' (possibly, the only part of the Prayer which our Lord originated), over and above its more obvious meaning, has a special interest, which remarkably coincides with the present argument. Like the first word 'Our,' the use of the plural number connects the prayer in a most vivid way with that precept of the Law which is a summary of the second Table, 'Thou shalt love thy neighbour as thyself.' The praying for our neighbour side by side with ourselves; the always saying 'our,' and 'us,' and 'we,' instead of 'mine,' and 'me,' and 'I,' is the fulfilment of this precept in a practical form. But as if to show that the second clause of the prayer corresponds particularly to the second Table of the Law, we have in this second clause the definite recognition of our neighbour's claims upon us. We naturally love our own souls, and pray that their stains may be blotted out in the Blood of Christ; but our Lord teaches us to pray that this mercy may be extended to us only so far as we extend it to our brother. How could the great Legislator of Sinai, who is also the great Prophet of the Sermon on the Mount, more emphatically reiterate His own precept, 'Thou shalt love thy neighbour as thyself'?

But if God should extend forgiveness to us without at the same time bestowing upon us His Grace, what would be the inevitable result? That we should fall into sin again; and, as the sin would be in this case sin against mercy received, we should need a larger and more liberal forgiveness. Therefore, from the suit for forgiveness we pass on, by a very natural connexion of ideas, to a suit for preservation from trial, if that may be. 'Forgive us our trespasses,

And lead us not into temptation.' But then this may *not* be always. It is God's will that His people should breathe all their life long an atmosphere of temptation. 'I pray not,' said Christ, 'that thou shouldest take them out of the world'; and what is the world but the very scene and theatre of trial? The soldiers of Christ, by the express will of their Captain, are not to be put out of harm's way; they are to be ever on the field of action, where bullets are flying and shells exploding. If then God will not always secure them from danger, what can He be asked to do for them? To secure them in danger (or to use our inimitable paraphrase again, 'that He will save and defend us in all dangers, ghostly and bodily'). We do not pray that He will take us out of action; but that He will keep the bullets from striking us. Here then is the significance of this 'But'—'Place us not in such trial as shall be an overmatch for our strength; suffer us not to be tempted above that we are able.'

'*But and if* Thou art pleased to suffer it, shield us from harm by Thy Grace.'

So end the petitions. And in the ascription of praise which is as a beautiful finial of the Prayer, we throw our eyes upwards once more, to assure ourselves in the confidence of faith, that God, in consideration of His excellence and greatness, will grant our petitions; we venture to remind Him that His interests are concerned in doing so. We are assured that Thou wilt help us, O God; Thou art concerned in helping us, O God; '*For* Thine is the Kingdom, and the power, and the glory.'

Thus is the Lord's Prayer a seed of prayer, containing in germ every petition which the human heart can send up to God, even as the Decalogue is a seed of precept, containing in germ every rule which can be given for human conduct. The great marvel in both is their comprehensiveness and brevity, the extraordinary organization and arrangement, the reduction of the subject treated to a few fundamental elements, manifested in those ten short precepts, in these seven short petitions.

And thus shines out the ineffable superiority of God's own work! No human mind at any period of civilization, however advanced, would be competent to draw up either the Decalogue or the Prayer. Everything that man does, you can exhaust; but this code and this prayer, cannot be exhausted; there is in them the power of an endless life. And the finger of God can be traced in their perfect simplicity and unostentatiousness. Uninspired man might perhaps draw up a more high-sounding prayer, seeming richer in its tones of pathos and devotion, than our Lord has done. But uninspired prayer, though abundant in colour, and sparkle, and rhetoric, would lack the grave simplicity of this Divine composition. A clever craftsman can make an artificial flower, which shall seem to a superficial observer even more blooming and more delicately painted than the flowers of Nature: but no craftsman can make a seed, with an imprisoned germ, which shall in due time become a flower, and contain in itself a power of endless reproduction. The production of such a seed, and the composition of the Lord's Prayer, we must leave to the Wisdom of God.

Would that we could always say the Lord's Prayer in perfect sincerity! The most we can do is to approximate to such a recitation of it. Oh what filial confidence in God does it imply! what regard for God's glory; what solicitude for our brother's welfare! Then all we dare hope is, to be able to say it with a little more of heart and sincerity to-morrow than to-day ; or next year, if God spares us, than this. And this will not be without acting it, as well as praying it. Let us pray then that we may act it, and by acting it work it into the texture of our minds.

> 'Only, O Lord, in Thy dear love
> Fit us for perfect rest above;
> And help us, this and every day,
> To live more nearly as we pray.'

CHAPTER II

THE CONTEXT OF THE LORD'S PRAYER

ONE of the indispensable rules for rightly understanding any passage of Holy Scripture is to look at the context in which it occurs. The more noteworthy passages, indeed all passages, grow up out of their context as one plant out of a group. There is a train of thought which leads up to them, and also a train of thought to which they lead up, which it is necessary to seize, if we would make ourselves masters of their true meaning. The Lord's Prayer, as given through St. Matthew, occurs in the Sermon on the Mount. In this section of the sermon our Lord instructs His disciples that prayer is to be offered secretly, and not with ostentation, as the Jews too often offered it;

and that the heathen mistake with regard to it, of repeating petitions over and over again, as if He whom we address did not know what we need before we ask Him, is also to be avoided. Then, because in an exercise of such immense importance, an exercise which is the soul's very breath of life, it is necessary to have very special guidance, He constructs for His disciples a perfect model of prayer. He appears to design it chiefly for private use; for He had just been speaking of entering into the closet and shutting the door when prayer is to be made. And yet the adoption of the plural throughout, the 'our' and the 'us,' seems to comprehend the congregation of faithful men as the secondary sphere, at any rate, for which the prayer is adapted.

But how is the Lord led up to speak of prayer at all? In the Beatitudes, with which the sermon opens, He describes the spirit and temper which should animate His disciples generally, and then warns them that, while the old platform of the Law and the Prophets would still remain standing, as the basis of all moral duty, a higher and more spiritual standard of obedience would be required of them in order to their entering into the kingdom of heaven, than that which was exhibited by the Scribes and Pharisees. The sixth commandment, for example, as it must be understood by them, would forbid not homicide only, but the railing and reviling words which might lead to it; the seventh would forbid the lustful look as well as the impure act, and so forth.

Next in order to moral duties (and inextricably associated with them) are religious observances. Nor let any man dare to put asunder what Almighty God hath closely joined together, morality and religion, or pretend that one can subsist without the other. Religious observances are three, and enumerated in an order which, like everything else in this sermon, is full of significance—Almsgiving, Prayer, Fasting. These religious observances represent respectively that threefold division of duty which St. Paul traces out (though in a different order) in his Epistle to Titus, 'that we should live soberly, righteously, and godly, in this present world.' Almsgiving represents our duty to our neighbour as a religious observance. It embraces (when understood in a large sense) every endeavour to help, relieve, or benefit, our neighbour; it is the outcome and expression of love to our neighbour, which is the essence of righteous living. But why should almsgiving be named first? Not surely because it is more important than prayer; but possibly because this is the order in which experience presents to us our duties. The first things that a child becomes conscious of are visible persons outside it, interested in it, and upon whom it is dependent—in Scriptural phrase, its 'neighbours.' As intelligence begins to dawn, and the idea of God, His law, His love, His heavenly home from which man strayed through sin, is thrown into the child's mind, in all the freshness of its faculties, when the dews of the baptismal birth lie glistening upon the soul, the first idea of duty is its duty to its neighbour.

And as almsgiving is the religious observance which represents our duty to our neighbour, so prayer (in the wide sense of the word embracing every exercise of devotion) is the observance which represents our duty to God—that we should live 'godly.'

Lastly, as our duty towards our neighbour is represented by the observance of almsgiving, and our duty to God by that of prayer, so our duty to ourselves ('that we should live soberly') is represented by fasting, this too being understood in the wide sense of self-discipline and self-control in whatever form it is exercised.

We have then before us the three great observances of religion with the instructions of Christ as to the method of fulfilling them; the method being secrecy in each case, with the view of securing that the motive shall be to please God, and not to win the praise of men. Prayer holds the central position, having as it were on its right hand almsgiving, and on its left fasting. And the central position is the most dignified and important, and that which most attracts regard; even as it was upon Calvary—'on either side one, and Jesus in the midst.'

While considering this part of the setting of

the Lord's Prayer, it is well to observe the connexion of the word 'when,' which appears three times, once in connexion with each observance; *when* thou doest alms; *when* thou prayest; *when* thou fastest.

Those who desire to evade the obligation of fasting, which the Sermon certainly seems to lay upon Christians, are apt to allege that our Lord does not actually bid His disciples fast, but only gives them a rule to be secret in their fasting, when they think it profitable to practise that observance. An unfortunate argument, for purposes of evasion, as it would equally apply to almsgiving and prayer, which no one would evade. For, as far as this passage goes, Christ does not bid His disciples either to give alms or pray, but merely says, 'when thou doest alms,' 'when thou prayest,' be careful not to let the pious action transpire or get abroad, it being assumed by Him that His disciples will certainly practise all these observances, and that all they will need is to be put on their guard against ostentation in practising them. And why might our Lord safely assume this? how is the assumption in keeping with the fundamental hypothesis upon which the Sermon on the Mount is based? Because the hearers were not persons ignorant of true religion, but more or less educated, trained, disciplined, in the knowledge of the system of Jewish religion. Almsgiving, prayer, and fasting, would be duties well known to them, as being often referred to in the Law and the writings of the Prophets, and inculcated upon them orally by those expositors of the Scriptures, the Scribes, who sate in Moses' seat. Accordingly, our Lord avowedly takes His stand upon the pre-existing foundation of the Law, as already laid in the mind of the hearers, and does not even pretend to teach anything strictly new, and which was not contained implicitly in the Scriptures of the earlier dispensation. Thus the assumptions made by the 'whens' are merely in pursuance of the warning He had already given, that He was not come to destroy the Law and the Prophets, but to fulfil.

The next point is to discern in the juxtaposition of the three duties their close and vital connexion with one another. For, seeing that they represent respectively our duty to our neighbour, our duty to God, and our duty to ourselves, must they not be closely and vitally connected? Our relations lie at the root and foundation of our duties; and the relation in which we stand to God as our Father involves and carries with it our relation to men as our brethren. Where there is more than one child in a family, the filial relation must necessarily involve the fraternal, and as there is a duty towards the father, so is there a duty also, though of a different kind, towards the brothers and sisters. Moreover, the Law of Moses, in laying down the duty of a man towards his neighbour, implicitly recognized his duty to himself. For the fundamental duty towards our neighbour, as stated in the Law, is, 'Thou shalt love thy neighbour as thyself'; and if thy neighbour as thyself, then thyself also as thy neighbour. Perhaps to the ears of some of us the words 'love of self' or 'self-love' have an ugly and ominous sound, as if they meant the same thing as selfishness. You may even see in spiritual books, which counsel high perfection, such phrases of pietism as this: 'Never, till we get rid of self-love altogether, shall we love God with the all-absorbing affection which is due to Him.' Bishop Butler ought to have put to flight for ever, from the minds of English Christians at all events, views so contrary to the true philosophy of our nature, and what is worse, so utterly unscriptural. It is in truth because men love and value themselves so little, according to the true estimate of what they are, because they care so little for their souls, made in God's image, and redeemed by Christ's blood, and study so little their own eternal interests, that so many of them are lost. And as to the notion that perfect disenthralment from self-love is essential to the highest type of character, are we not told that our Lord, in whom was no sin, 'for the joy that was set before Him endured the cross, despising the shame'? To what motive in the human heart would the joy that was set before Him make an appeal but to self-love? And if almsgiving, prayer, and fasting, as representing the threefold division of human duty, are closely welded together, and presented to us by the Divine Legislator in His Sermon on the Mount in combination with one another, is it not quite possible that what so often blocks our prayers, and shuts them out at present from success, may be that there is in our lives a deficiency of the observances which our Lord groups together with prayer, and thus a putting asunder of things which God hath joined together?

And first, may there not be a deficiency in our alms? in other words, in recognizing the claims of God and of our neighbours upon our substance? Are those claims honestly and fairly satisfied, and do we make it a point of conscience to ascertain that we are satisfying them, doing as much for works of piety and charity as we are bound to do? Indeed, without this all professions of sympathy and devotion are so much hypocrisy and self-deceit. It is just that saying to the hungry and destitute, 'Depart in peace, be ye warmed and filled,' which St. James withers with his inspired sarcasm. Nor can any man satisfy his own conscience that he is doing his duty in the matter of almsgiving unless he gives upon system, settling first between God and his own conscience what amount he ought to give, and then by means of an ordinary debtor and creditor account ascertaining that that amount is really given year by year.

The proportion of a man's substance specified in Scripture as that which is due to God, and upon which He has a claim, is one-tenth of the whole. It is true that this proportion is mentioned only in the Old Testament, and that in the New we have no more definite guidance on the subject than our Lord's strong implication, in what He says about the widow's mite, that it is the amount, not of the gift itself, but of the self-denial which appears in it, which makes it acceptable to God. But on the other hand, it is to be taken into consideration that, as in the case of fasting, the Gospel dispensation stands upon the dispensation which preceded it, and that there is reason therefore to think that requirements of the old dispensation not expressly abolished (as the whole Jewish ritual is) are in force still. Moreover, this proportion of a tenth as God's due stands quite clear of the Law of Moses, recognized as it was by the patriarchs Abraham and Jacob, long before the giving of the Law. It may indeed be alleged with great show of reason that a tenth to a man of very large means would represent no sacrifice at all, while to one in very straitened circumstances the giving of a tenth would involve considerable self-denial, — a self-denial which might cut him to the quick. But *all* the restrictions of God's law are more difficult of observance to some classes of people than others, and yet this circumstance cannot be held to release any class from those restrictions. It is doubtless far harder to bridle one's sinful lusts at eighteen, than at eighty; but that fact does not exempt the youth of eighteen, any more than the man of eighty, from the obligation of bridling his sinful lusts. Similarly, though it be true that two pounds a year given to God out of an income of only twenty pounds represents a considerable self-denial, whereas a thousand a year out of an income of ten thousand represents but little, still it does not follow that

The Context of the Lord's Prayer

God may not require the man who has but twenty pounds to give Him annually two of them for works of charity and piety. At all events these two positions may be advanced with certainty, and do not admit of question or controversy,—first, that every one is solemnly bound (as a distinct religious obligation) to give to God a certain proportion of what he possesses; and secondly, that no mere giving out of our abundance, and what we do not feel the want of, satisfies the requirement that the proportion must be such as to involve self-denial.

Then as to fasting, do we join it with prayer? if not in the literal sense of periodical total abstinence from food (which possibly in some cases might be found prejudicial to health), yet at all events in the form of stern self-discipline and self-control, as e. g. in sleep, in amusements and recreations, in the time given to light reading, in the general management of our time. The high-wrought civilization, of which we are apt to make so great a boast, has brought with it an amount of cheap resources and refinements and a general softness of habits, hitherto unprecedented in the history of our country. We are surrounded on all sides by contrivances to save trouble, to remove petty annoyances, to make life as much as possible a bed of eider-down. And one result of all this softness and luxury (as it always has been in the history of nations) is dissoluteness of morals. God will have His people make a firm protest against such a state of things, by setting an example of self-discipline and self-control. A little stern it will need to be sometimes, not only to stem the stream of tendency in the opposite direction, but also to keep under in each Christian the sinful lusts of the flesh, so apt to be pampered and made exacting and insatiate by the comforts and luxuries which an advanced civilization furnishes. 'Thou therefore endure hardness, as a good soldier of Jesus Christ' (2 Tim. ii. 3). Are we in any sense or form enduring hardness? are we animated in reference to the spiritual warfare which is being waged on the earth, with anything of the brave Hittite's spirit? 'The ark, and Israel, and Judah, abide in tents;

and my lord Joab, and the servants of my lord, are encamped in the open fields; shall I then go into mine house, to eat and to drink?' (2 Sam. xi. 11). It may be—nay, it is more than possible, it is probable—that our prayers are shut out from their legitimate effect because our lives are so wanting in moral stamina, so easy, so self-indulgent, so absolutely devoid of that self-denial which is the salt of the spiritual character. One more element of vital connexion between the three great observances may be traced in the fact that fasting, rightly and wisely conducted, is a practical furtherance towards the practice of the other two. It is a furtherance to prayer, because real and cordial prayer demands the highest amount of mental energy, and this is seriously impeded by undue indulgence of bodily appetites. It is a furtherance to almsgiving, inasmuch as the means for indulgence, when saved from that channel of expenditure, may supply no small contribution to a man's charitable purse.

CHAPTER III

THE SOURCES OF THE LORD'S PRAYER

WAS Christianity a new religion, of which our blessed Lord was the originator? Or was it not rather a new development of the one old true religion, which had subsisted ever since the creation of man, and upon which the hopes of all God's saints and servants both in the patriarchal and Jewish dispensations had been nourished? If there were absolutely no alternative between these propositions, we should rather affirm the latter than the former of them. But the fact is, that in each of them there is an element of truth. In a certain sense, and under a certain aspect of it, Christianity is new. In another sense, and under another aspect of it, it is old. This is what St. John says of the precept to love one another, which is one of the two great precepts of the Gospel[1]. It was in one sense an old commandment, which the Church of God had received and possessed from the beginning. It dated long before Christ, for Christ referred back to it when He said: 'The first of all the commandments is, Hear, O Israel; the Lord our God is one Lord: and thou shalt love the Lord thy God with all thy heart, soul, mind, strength: this is the first commandment. And the second is like, namely this, Thou shalt love thy neighbour as thyself.' It is found in so many words in the nineteenth chapter of the Book of Leviticus; and though not expressed in writing before Moses, it was graven upon man's heart from the beginning. It condemned (we may be very sure) the murder of Abel. And yet in another sense the commandment was 'new,' and originated with Christ. He lit it up with the illustration of His

---

[1] I write no new commandment unto you, but an old commandment which ye had from the beginning. The old commandment is the word which ye heard. Again, a new commandment I write unto you, which thing is true in Him and in you: because the darkness is passing away, and the true Light already shineth.'—1 John ii. 7, 8.

example, laying down His life for us, and teaching us as the primary precept of His Gospel that we ought also to lay down our lives for the brethren. What a new force and significance did this give to the precept! Let us imagine a beautiful transparency; a picture traced by a master-hand upon a material capable of transmitting the light. Let us suppose that with a considerable number of other transparencies, painted originally with a certain reference to it—say to form side-scenes to it, or backgrounds, or skies—it is allowed to lie about in a lumber-room, the owner being ignorant what an artistic treasure he possesses. And then suppose that one day, a clearance being made of the lumber-room, it is discovered that the pictures are transparencies, and it is resolved to exhibit them as such. Bright lights in a darkened chamber are placed behind the frames of them, and then the beauty of the main scene is immediately appreciated and admired. And more than this. The minor transparencies are found out to be parts of the same design. Each has its place in forming one great picture. The light placed behind the transparencies reveals not only beauty in them, but order, harmony, and coherence. Now in the supposed case, is the scene so much admired an old scene or a new one? Substantially old. It has been in existence for many a long year. But virtually, and as regards its treatment, and its effect upon the beholders, it is a newly-found treasure. Now this is the image under which St. John tells us that we should look at the relation between Christianity and the forms of true religion which went before it. The precepts, and even the doctrines, of Christianity were in existence before Christ came, but they were dark, and in confusion, incapable of being fully, truly, and consistently appreciated. Christ, when He appeared and fulfilled the marvellous career which prophecy had traced out for Him, placed a light behind them. And the light was Himself, in His person, in His example, in His doctrine, in His precept. It is not true that before Christ there was no revelation of human immortality. The doctrine of a future state is one, in the absence of which no real religion can exist in the heart of any man; and we have the assurance of the inspired writer to the Hebrews that the patriarchs desired 'a better country, that is, an heavenly'—that Abraham in particular 'looked for a city which hath foundations, whose builder and maker is God' (Heb. xi. 10, 16). But it was reserved for our Lord, the first-begotten from the dead, to bring life and immortality to light, and to illuminate with glorious hopes the prospect beyond the grave; and therefore before Him immortality was rather insinuated in the inspired Scriptures, than expressly stated; it was spoken of with bated breath, whispered in the ear in closets, not proclaimed upon housetops. And I need not add (because that is so obvious) that the whole elaborate system of sacrifice, both eucharistic and atoning (which is clearly traceable up to the times of our first parents, whose sons practised it), received its illustration and explanation from our Lord's life of self-devotion and atoning death, that He was the true Light which gave significance and beauty to those old ritual shadows, and which is seen through them when we look at them from the Christian point of view.

These general reflections have been handled somewhat at length, because the origin of the Lord's Prayer is in fact determined by them. Did this blessed and beautiful Prayer originate with Christ or not? In a certain sense No. God had a Church, hoping in a foreseen Christ, before the Word was made flesh and dwelt among us. Now in this Church all, or nearly all, the rudiments of the Lord's Prayer are found. The devotional literature of Israel furnishes at all events parallels to each petition, and in some cases the express words of which our Lord was pleased to make use. This has been fully exhibited by Dr. John Lightfoot in his *Miscellanies*, ch. 20[1]. But in order to appreciate this fact rightly, it must be remembered that even before the appearance of Christ, the Church of God was under the guidance of

---

[1] This great master of Hebrew learning must not be confounded with Bishop Joseph Lightfoot of Durham, an eminent Greek scholar of our own generation.—B. C.

Christ's Spirit. St. Peter expressly ascribes this guidance to the prophets: 'Searching what, or what manner of time the Spirit of Christ which was in them did signify' (1 Pet. i. 11). St. Paul ascribes to the whole people of Israel during their pilgrimage in the wilderness a certain sacramental connexion with Christ; 'for they drank,' says he, 'of that spiritual Rock that followed them; and *that Rock was Christ*' (1 Cor. x. 4).

It is not therefore so true or so reverent to say that Christ, in framing the Lord's Prayer, availed Himself of materials made ready to His hand, as that He took up again certain devout utterances which His own Spirit had already inspired. He places them in a new light, and gives them a new illustration in connexion with His own work and teaching. If in a certain sense we must say that the Lord's Prayer is framed of previously existing materials, in another sense we must admit it to be new. The germs of all things were in the chaos, in those dark waters on whose face the Spirit of God brooded; but this is no drawback to the

The Sources of the Lord's Prayer 43

wonderfulness of the process of creation, by which all things were reduced into order and method of arrangement, the light being separated from the darkness, and the firmament from the earth, and the sea from the dry land, and firmament and earth and sea being stocked respectively with bodies celestial, terrestrial, and aquatic. The Lord's Prayer is a magnificent creation by the Divine Wisdom which dwelt in Christ, out of elements previously existing, but confused; a creation in which He methodizes and systematizes prayer, reduces it under its primary heads, and with a wonderful grasp of the subject comprehends the whole of it in the hollow of His hand.

But in addition to this, the example, work, and teaching of Christ shed a wholly new light upon, and presented under an entirely new aspect, petitions which existed indeed, but could be little appreciated, before His appearance.

Thus e.g. an ancient Jewish prayer begins with the invocation of the Lord's Prayer in so many words: 'Our Father which art in Heaven.' This exordium was strictly in accordance with the Scriptures of the Old Testament; for in them the nation of Israel is distinctly recognized as standing in the filial relation to God: 'Thus saith the Lord, Israel is *My son*, even My *firstborn*' (Exod. iv. 22). And again: 'Do ye thus requite the Lord, O foolish people and unwise? is not He *thy Father that hath bought thee?*' (Deut. xxxii. 6). And again: 'I am *a Father to Israel*, and Ephraim *is My firstborn*' (Jer. xxxi. 9). And again: 'Doubtless *Thou art our Father*, though Abraham be ignorant of us, and Israel acknowledge us not: Thou, O Lord, *art our Father*, our Redeemer' &c. (Is. lxiii. 16). But what a totally new force and significance does the Christian revelation give to the appeal, 'Our Father which art in Heaven'! A national and natural sonship was all that the Jew could claim, in conformity with his Scriptures: 'Israel is My son ... I am a Father to Israel.' He had never been addressed in these terms: 'Behold, what manner of love the Father hath bestowed upon us, that we should be called' (not collectively or nationally or naturally, but personally and individually and supernaturally), the 'sons of God ... Beloved, now are we the sons of God' (1 John iii. 1, 2). Of the deep mystery of man's supernatural adoption into God's family nothing could have been known till Christ came to effectuate and to explain it. Christ, God's Son from everlasting, the Second Person in the ever-blessed Trinity, took flesh, that is to say, assumed human nature without any distinct human personality, and thus became Son of Man, in order that He might ally Himself with all men, and qualify Himself to represent all. This is the foundation of the mystery. Holy Baptism, duly administered, incorporates us into Christ, gives us a real connexion with the humanity of the second Adam, as by natural generation we have a real connexion with the humanity of the first. Christ therefore being not only in His divine nature the Son of God, but also in His humanity having been conceived by the Holy Ghost and born of the Virgin Mary, we, by our incorporation into Him, effected by the Sacrament of Baptism, become God's children by adoption and grace. Each of us in turn and singly becomes so; for Baptism is an ordinance administered to each individually, and quite irrespectively of race or extraction. It seals an individual, not a national, privilege. But now throw all this doctrine respecting the representative humanity of the Son of God and our connexion with it into the old Jewish invocation, 'Our Father which art in heaven,' and with what a new and holy lustre does it light up this venerable form of address! Familiar as the words might have been to the ears of a Jew in our Lord's time, we may say of them, as they are illuminated with Christian doctrine and association, 'Thou hast put a new song in my mouth.' When Christ, the Son of Man no less than the Son of God, is seen behind and through them, representing us before the throne of God, and bidding and encouraging the humblest of the children of Abraham after the promise, to call God Father, they are no more the same words, or rather, while they are the same in sound, they are different in sense. Like the lineaments of our Lord's natural body, when He took up the three disciples into a high mountain apart, they are transfigured. A beautiful and attractive glory pervades them, which they never had before. Old in the letter, they are new in the spirit.

We might go through the other parts of the Lord's Prayer, and show how in nearly all the petitions the terms employed are drawn from Jewish forms of devotion, and yet how everywhere those terms borrow quite a new force from the revelations and doctrines of Christianity. We may therefore say generally that in one sense the Prayer is old, in another new; its rudiments were in existence long before it was framed; but it has a spirit and a life which did not appear in the rudiments, just as the blossom has a spirit and a life which does not appear in the bud, and as the butterfly has a spirit and a life which does not appear in the cocoon.

In short, this Prayer is part and parcel of the Christian religion. And the Christian religion in all its essential parts, in its doctrines, in its precepts, in its rites, in its forms of devotion, is a beautiful blossom which unfolded itself out of the bud of the religion of the Old Covenant.

There is perhaps no one feature of modern religious thought more characteristic than its impatience of everything old, its craving for novelty. This craving is in the air just now; we all inhale it more or less into our mental and moral system. Never was there a greater impatience of solid theological works, and solid sermons, which set forth old and well-established truth in Scriptural and primitive formularies. Our readers and our congregations must have some fare which stimulates the jaded appetite. If solid nourishment is ever tolerated by them, it must be dressed and served up in an entirely new form, and seasoned with some new condiment; and often it will happen that where the nourishment is entirely wanting, the condiment alone serves the turn; something questionably sound, if it be only smart and flippant, is relished and finds acceptance. With prophetic insight the Apostle Paul foresaw that it would be so. 'The time will come,' predicted he, 'when they will not endure sound doctrine; but after their own lusts shall they heap to themselves teachers, *having itching ears*' (2 Tim. iv. 3). And never surely—whatever be the secondary causes which have contributed to bring about the result, whether it be the mental stir prevalent among us on the subject of religion, the rapid rate at which civilization develops itself, the spread of elementary religious knowledge, and the familiarity of almost all with the rudiments of the faith, or all these causes combined—never was there a greater appetite for novelty, never was the antiquated more generally distasteful. It is forgotten too that for those Church people who have received a fair religious education, edification is not so much promoted by instilling truth in any new form, as by reminding them of what they already know; according to that profound word of St. Peter's, 'Wherefore I will not be negligent to put you always in remembrance of these things, *though ye know them*, and be stablished in the present truth' (2 Pet. i. 12).

Another symptom of the love of novelty now abroad is the craving for an additional tincture of imagination in scriptural narratives and biographies. To please readers in this day, a man must write not so much accurately and truthfully, as pictorially and with scenic effect. We are impatient of the dull matters of fact of history and biography; we ask for the introduction of a poetic element; that the history should become an historical drama, the biography an historical romance. If we care at all for seeing Christ, we would fain see Him under a new aspect; we desire (as we say in our own defence) to *realize* Him—not however with the realization of faith, but with that sort of artificial realization which the imaginative faculty can give. A picture of him in the mind—this is what we really desiderate; and we care not overmuch if, in painting this picture, the author uses the licence conceded to writers of romance, and deals somewhat cavalierly with the facts. Alas! if the interest and fascination of such writing cannot be denied, at how small a fraction must we compute the edification to be derived from it. The old in theology is to be made new, not by touching it up with the pencil and brush of the imagination, and then putting the antique painting into a modern frame, but by simply accepting the old well-worn truths of Creed and Catechism, and with deep heart-searching and prayer trying to see their applicability to the ever-new emergencies of our own inner life.

Finally, the craving after a sensational worship grows out of the same morbid habit of mind, and is another symptom of the general complaint under which, because it is in the air, we all more or less labour. The Church Services in their old form pall upon us; they have become to us, in process of time, dull, stale, flat, and unprofitable. We try to make them lively and to give them interest; and so far well. But alas! the interest which we seek to throw into these Services is chiefly derived from externals. Instead of endeavouring to perceive the intrinsic beauty of the Services in the first instance, in which case the appropriateness and meaning of the sober ritual of the Catholic Church would become apparent as we proceeded, we begin with externals because externals strike the eye or the ear (and so cannot but produce a certain impression), and making these always more and more florid, we too often end by substituting a spectacle or a musical entertainment for the worship of God in spirit and in truth. But surely our subject teaches us a different lesson respecting the method of communicating interest to the Services of the Church. All these Services have upon them the stamp of primitive antiquity. But does their age at all deprive them of their force, their beauty, their significance? We believe it to be just the reverse. We believe that in these old forms (even as in the Lord's own Prayer in a much higher degree) there is an exhaustless and ever-fresh applicability, making them words for all time, for all generations of Christians, for all circumstances of the Church. What makes them seem stale to so many of us is, that we do not really know them, have never studied them; that while their sound is in our ear, their sense is not in our heart. It is possible that, when our Lord gave to the disciple who said, 'Lord, teach us to pray,' the priceless form known as the Lord's Prayer, some little feeling of disappointment may have been

The Sources of the Lord's Prayer 53

experienced by the applicant for instruction. 'And is this all He has to give us? I have heard most of those words before in synagogue-worship, in the devotions issued by great rabbis for the use of their scholars. I anticipated something fresher, newer, more animating, couched not in the old stereotyped devotional phraseology.' If he secretly reasoned thus, it was simply because he had yet never dived under the surface of the phraseology, but merely skimmed it, like a seabird on the wing. Hundreds do the same with the Offices of the Book of Common Prayer. With a laudatory fashion of talking about 'our incomparable liturgy,' they combine a profound ignorance of what is in it. They have never mastered the rationale or got an insight into the significance of a single Office of the Church. They have merely heard the Office used; and have taken up with the popular acceptance or the popular censure of it (both equally shallow). To give a single instance where a thousand might be given; who is there that has not heard the Burial Service read several times? And how many, even of those who have heard it very often, have any idea that in the three opening sentences there is a beautiful reference to the order in which the funeral procession enters the church? The first sentence being the voice of the Saviour, represented by the priest who leads the procession, 'I am the Resurrection and the Life, saith the Lord'; the second being the voice of the dead, who is borne into the church immediately after the priest, 'I know that my Redeemer liveth,' &c.; and the third being the voice of the mourners, reflecting on the transitoriness of worldly wealth and glory, and resigning themselves to God's will under their bereavement, 'We brought nothing into this world, and it is certain we can carry nothing out. The Lord gave, and the Lord hath taken away; blessed be the Name of the Lord.'

Far better than any external condiment of music and colour and gesture is the deep understanding of the true inner meaning of our Services, at once old and new. This condiment is ever fresh, never palls upon the devout worshipper. Then the Light which shined of old in darkness (though the darkness of ignorance could not wholly envelop it), will shine out, will transfigure the old words with the newness of the spirit, though still in the oldness of the letter. 'Because the darkness is passing away, and the true Light already shineth.'

CHAPTER IV

THE TWO RECORDS OF THE LORD'S PRAYER

We may conclude with great probability that those incidents or discourses which are recorded more than once in the Gospels are thus repeated on account of their transcendent importance. We know for certain that the Death and Resurrection of Christ, as being the events upon which all the hopes of humanity are suspended, are the most important incidents of the Gospel history. And, of His Death and Resurrection we have four different accounts from four different pens, whereas the less significant events of His career are passed over by some of the Evangelists in silence; the Transfiguration being recorded by only three of them, the Nativity, the Infancy, and the Ascension by two only, and the striking incident of the childhood only by one. This circumstance alone furnishes strong presumptive evidence that the repetition of certain Gospel narratives proceeds upon principle, and that the principle is the superior importance of the event or discourse of which we have several reports.

This Divine Prayer was first given in the course of the Sermon on the Mount, as recorded by St. Matthew. Our Lord, in fulfilment of the prediction that He should be a prophet like unto Moses, was legislating for His Church while He gave it; and this Prayer enters into, and forms part of, the legislative code, and is solemnly placed by Him upon the statute-book of Christianity. He is giving rules, or rather announcing principles, for three religious exercises which were often practised (as by the centurion Cornelius) in conjunction with one another—almsgiving, prayer, and fasting. In the performance of these exercises, He says, we are not to court publicity, as the Pharisaic hypocrites of the day did, but rather to shun the eye of men, and seek only the approbation of Him who seeth in secret. Prayer especially is to be offered with closed doors in the privacy of our closet. And as Jewish ostentation is to be entirely eschewed in private devotion, so also is that babbling and vain repetition of the heathens, which proceeded on the idea that God needs to be made acquainted with our wants, and that much speaking will succeed in attracting His attention. Upon this last piece of advice the Lord's Prayer immediately follows. It is connected with the warning against vain repetitions by the conjunction, 'Therefore'; 'After this manner pray ye.' As much as to say, 'I have warned you how you are *not* to pray; now therefore let Me show you how you are to pray.' The connexion established by this 'therefore' is of the closest kind. For the more we study the Lord's Prayer, the more we are struck by its exceeding terseness, by the entire absence of the superfluous and redundant. The minutest particle, as we shall see in the sequel, contributes something to the meaning of the Prayer; not an 'and' or 'but' could be struck out without striking out an idea; and therefore the connexion of this Prayer with a warning against vain repetitions in prayer, is one of the most apposite sequences by which thought can be linked to thought.

But it would further appear from the preceding warning on the subject of privacy in prayer that our Lord on this occasion designed His Prayer for the use of His people in private devotion. It has indeed been contended by divines of no mean authority, and especially by the learned Dr. John Lightfoot, that on this, the first occasion of its utterance, the Prayer was designed as a form for *public* worship. But surely if this were the case, we should hardly have found in the same paragraph with the Prayer an express warning against praying in the synagogues and at the corners of the street, and an express precept to ensconce ourselves in our closets when we pray. To give the prayer in connexion with such a warning and precept must surely imply at least that it is a form suitable for private devotion, and approved by our Lord for that purpose. Not, of course, that it is the only form which may so be used. It is introduced by the direction, 'After this manner therefore pray ye,' which though it means primarily 'Use the actual words,' does also mean secondarily, 'Let this be your model in private prayer; pray thus tersely, thus pithily, thus comprehensively, directing your petitions by a mental reference to those which I have here laid down for you.'

But primarily the Lord will have us use the actual words as a permanent form of prayer. Forms of prayer are not really, as some suppose, a hindrance to the spirit of prayer in private devotion. The Lord's Prayer is not only a form, but a thoroughly studied and perfectly elaborated form, and yet, if the connexion in which it was given may be trusted, it is designed for use in the closet. Sound and scriptural forms of prayer are of the greatest use in our private moments of communion with God. They act as a check upon the mind in its tendency to wander; they tend to concentrate thought and to prevent diffuseness; as they have been considered and digested beforehand, there is less liability to go astray in them than when the mind trusts itself to the spontaneous effusions of the moment. But while the mind is restrained and chastened in its approaches to the Throne of Grace, there can be no reason why its freedom should be crippled. Let there be a platform in private prayer; the Lord's Prayer itself makes the best of platforms; but let us always consider ourselves at liberty to enlarge upon this platform, and to weave into the pre-conceived prayer new petitions, as often as we shall feel ourselves moved to do so. The aiming at this will prevent formality—a snare into which we are very liable to fall, if we never vary from a fixed routine of religious phraseology. The state of mind to be coveted and striven after in prayer is a state of restrained freedom—freedom to present any petition to God through our Redeemer's mediation and intercession, but freedom restrained by a deep reverence for Him whom we address, and also by the feeling that we know not what we should pray for as we ought, and that, if left to the impulses and reasonings of our own minds, we should often ask things either mischievous or unprofitable.

The second occasion of giving the Lord's Prayer was different in all its circumstances from the first, and occurred probably at an interval of more than two years from the Sermon on the Mount[1]. Our Lord was pray-

[1] In a sermon, or popular treatment of the Lord's Prayer, a discussion of the correctness of the view that the Lord's Prayer was given twice would be out of place. And the Dean states his own view without argument. There are dangers in accounting for a diversity of testimony in the relation of similar facts by the supposition of the independence of the facts. There are also dangers in the contrary direction, when shallow observers lose sight of one of the greatest and deepest principles of God's working, viz. the doing things at twice, with most significant variations on the two occasions. This latter dangerous tendency has more easily commended itself to less thoughtful people, and has often been the cause of unjustifiable accommodations of the original texts of the different Gospels, as well as the loss of the special lessons of the diversities in the narratives, such as are here pointed out by the Dean. In this particular case, St. Luke's record is imbedded in the midst of the great distinctive section of his Gospel, extending from ch. ix. 51 to ch. xviii. 15. This section contains the Church's only account of our Lord's ministry in Peraea, on His last journey up to Jerusalem, 'when the days were well-nigh come that He should be received up.'

When we remember that it was specially entrusted to St. Luke 'to trace the course of all things accurately from the very first, and write them in order,' it is hardly conceivable that such an Evangelist, with such a special commission of the Holy Ghost, should have confused with the circumstances of this last journey, and of the

ing in a certain place. We are not informed whether His prayer was vocal, as we know it was on some occasions (as for instance on the occasion recorded in the seventeenth chapter of St. John's Gospel), or mental. Anyhow, He was in the posture and attitude of prayer; it was evident to the disciples who were around Him that His whole soul was deeply engaged in it. They waited in reverential silence, not venturing to intrude upon His communion with His unseen Father till He had either risen from His knees, or, if standing, had seated Himself again. At length 'He ceased' praying[1]. When our Lord had risen from His prayer, one of His disciples, who had possibly been watching Him

Peraean ministry, a notable occurrence at the very commencement of the Galilaean ministry, following close upon the call of the Apostles.—B. C.

[1] This throws some light upon the Apostle's precept, 'Pray without ceasing;' 1 Thess. v. 17. To pray without ceasing cannot mean that we are always to be engaged in direct acts of prayer; for from these direct acts the Lord Himself, the great model of human duty, ceased. It cannot imply more than the maintenance of that calm self-recollected state of mind which flows from realizing the presence of God, and which habitually and instinctively refers to God amidst the trials and difficulties of daily life.

during the exercise, asked Him for a form of prayer (for such was the real significance of the request) such as the Jewish doctors were in the habit of giving to their scholars as a kind of watchword, to distinguish them from the scholars of other schools. John the Baptist had dictated to his disciples a form of this kind; and many of John the Baptist's disciples had, as we know, before this joined our Lord. Possibly this was one of them. And his asking for a form of prayer, long after a form had been given by Christ, may have arisen from the fact that he was a new convert, who had been but recently drawn into the ranks of Christ's followers. Our Lord replied by definitely giving as a form the same prayer (with a few variations) which He had before given as a model upon which all our prayers should be framed. He now binds upon His disciples the use of the actual words by the phrase with which on this occasion He introduces it: 'When ye pray, say.' The prayer, though substantially the same, is here presented to us in a different point of view, a point of view which is too often missed.

The Lord's Prayer is the watchword of Christ's faithful soldiers and servants, by the use of which, and by its general currency among them both in private and public devotion, they may be recognized as Christians. To adopt the language of our Church on a different subject, 'it is a sign of profession and mark of difference whereby Christian men are discerned from others.' And this accounts for its position in the Office for the Service of Public Baptism, where the recital of it is directed immediately after the Sacrament has been administered. No sooner is the new recruit formally admitted and registered under the banner of Christ, than the watchword of the Christian army is put into his mouth by being recited for him. And as the mere *verbal* employment of this watchword distinguishes professing Christians from Jews and heathens, so the *spiritual* use of it is a test which establishes a distinction between thorough and shallow Christians. 'If any man,' says St. Paul, 'have not the Spirit of Christ,' however much he may wear the livery of Christian profession, 'he is none of His.' Now the very Spirit of Christ breathes in this prayer; and therefore it serves to discriminate between those who are truly His and those who merely go under that name. Does your heart echo the words, 'Our Father,' &c.?

Can you and do you call God your Father, your reconciled Father, in confidence, reverence, and love? Are you zealous for His honour? are you seeking His kingdom? are you furthering and acquiescing in His will? In a word, can you say the Lord's Prayer with your heart as well as with your tongue? Then pass among the citizens of the heavenly Jerusalem as a friend. By this watchword thou hast fellowship with saints all over the world, however widely separated from them—by sea, and mountain-range, and long tracts of desert. By this watchword thou hast fellowship with the spirits of the departed righteous, who are waiting in paradise (as thou waitest upon earth) for the accomplishment of the number of God's elect, and the full coming of His kingdom. And when thou passest out of this body of humiliation, and art challenged by the angels as to the Captain under whom thou hast served, thou shalt by this watchword, recognizing God as thy reconciled Father in Christ Jesus, pass unharmed amid the serried host, and find admittance into paradise.

In the Gospel of the faithful companion of St. Paul, observe how by the example of prayer, which our blessed Lord set, the disciple was drawn in to seek counsel respecting prayer, to make inquiry respecting an exercise so obviously blessed and glorious. It must indeed have been an elevating sight to have seen our Lord in prayer, even if the prayer were mental only, and no words were audible. From the sinless purity of His human nature, and from the habitual intercourse which He held with the Father, one can imagine what must have been in prayer the solemn simplicity of His manner, the chastened fervour of His gestures, the illumination of His features. Almost every prayer of His, one would think, with the exception of that agonizing one in the garden, must have been a minor transfiguration, in which angelic forms, although invisible, must have seemed to be floating around Him. No wonder the spectacle of Christ's praying exerted a marked influence upon this disciple! We are not told that, when our Lord preached on the subject of prayer in the Sermon on the Mount, any inquirer was led to evince a special interest in the subject. But now, when He shows them by example how to pray, when He lifts up His eyes and His hands to the Father which is in heaven, the sight is so elevating, so unconsciously lifts the spectators above the earth, that they long to pray too. They become so impressed with the idea that prayer is a great and arduous work, that they ask with admirable simplicity what may be the right method of performing it. Our Lord's Prayers, of course, must stand on an eminence above all others, in respect of their influence both with God and men; still in less degree the same attraction towards prayer emanates from all who pray under the influence of Christ's Spirit and the guidance of Christ's example. And thus it is that in devout congregations, which throw themselves actively into the Services of the Church, respond heartily, kneel humbly, and sing with the spirit and with the understanding also, devotion becomes contagious, and spreads from soul to soul. The man who sauntered into the church listlessly, perhaps as a pastime on a wet afternoon, or perhaps bent merely upon listening to the sermon, without any design of personal worship, is struck and roused by the calm earnestness of the lips and faces around him, and by-and-by is drawn insensibly into the current of prayer and praise, and so falling down on his face worships God, and reports that God is indeed, as He has promised to be, in the midst of the two or three gathered together in His name.

It is a serious question for every congregation, how far is their worship likely to prove attractive to strangers who might casually witness it? Attractive it will prove, and must prove, if there be in it reality and earnestness; if, in short, it be, not the mere recital of a Liturgy, but a living communion of living souls with the living God. The soul of the most worldly-minded man is still quite susceptible of an influence from the spectacle of earnest devotion in others, quite capable of being so impressed by the sight of spiritual worship, that he is involuntarily drawn into saying to Him, who never refuses to instruct the ignorant, 'Lord, teach me also to pray.' If it be the part of ministers of God to teach men how to pray by precept, it is no less the people's part, as servants of God, to attract them towards prayer by example. Has the worship of our Church, each congregation may well ask, a tendency to do this? Is it stirring, rousing, edifying to the careless and worldly brother who sits amongst us? Or is it only, as, alas, it is in some churches, the payment of a formal homage, decorous in its external arrangements, like a corpse laid out for burial, but stone-cold and dead?

Secondly, how full of instruction is the circumstance that the inquirer on the subject of prayer is not presented with anything new, but referred to the same old form, which had been given two years ago! Our Lord thus virtually says to him, 'Everything which can be desired in order to secure the holiness of My people here and their happiness hereafter,

I have already summed up in one brief but most comprehensive form. I have nothing more to add to that form. Why would you have another? To study and thoroughly to master this, to say this Prayer not only by heart, but with the heart, is more than work enough for a lifetime.'

There are some who clamour for a new set of forms of public prayer, or (which is much the same thing in point of principle) for several fundamental variations and improvements in the old one. Now since the Prayer-book is uninspired, we may not for a moment maintain that, like the Lord's Prayer, it is incapable of improvement. But this we may and do say, that in the Common Prayer, with which God has blessed this Church of England, there is a vast mine of theological and devotional treasure, which most of those who clamour for its improvement have scarcely at all explored. Who has studied the Prayer-book carefully, thoughtfully, with an earnest desire to appreciate the rationale of its arrangements, and with even a moderate furniture of sound learning? Is there one such person, who, however he may acknowledge flaws here and there, is not on the whole abundantly contented with the Prayer-book? And as for those who have given the Prayer-book no study at all, why would they have another Form of Prayer before they have mastered the full significance of this? Very much as St. Philip said to the eunuch, 'Understandest thou what thou readest?' so we may say to the majority of professing Churchmen, 'Understandest thou what thou prayest?' The words have been in your ears so constantly that they have ceased to make an impression on the mind. Have you ever sought to go below the surface of them? have you ever striven to realize them? have you ever even asked seriously what they mean?

Ah! it is not new forms of prayer which we stand in need of; but new affections to animate the old forms. It is a spiritual impulse, not a verbal variation, which is needed to give men a living interest in these old prayers. When his heart is touched with the sense of any recent mercy, with what fervour will a man say the General Thanksgiving; and what unction will there seem to him to be in the words! When the burden of the sins of his youth presses heavily upon his conscience, how will the Confession in the Communion Service—'The remembrance of them is grievous unto us; the burden of them is intolerable'—seem to him the exact expression of his needs! Offer him a new form of Public Service *then*, when his mind has conformed itself to the keynote of the old form, and what is the result? 'Straightway he saith, The old is better.'

Let the docility too of this disciple be a subject for our imitation. 'Lord,' said he, realizing his own incapacity to pray as the Lord prayed,—' Lord, teach us to pray.' Prayer is a very arduous exercise; and if we trust to the guidance of our own spirits in it, how easily may we be misled. It would seem at first sight as if nothing could be more honourably ambitious, or could betoken a higher degree of faith, than for two brothers to pray, in the days of Christ's humiliation upon earth, 'Grant that we may sit, the one on Thy right hand and the other on Thy left, in Thy kingdom.'

Yet the prayer was repulsed; it did not meet with favour or acceptance. Again, it seemed to St. Paul very desirable that he should no longer be tried by the thorn in the flesh; but when he besought the Lord thrice that it might depart from him, the terms of the refusal made him feel that the petition had not been a wise one. It was better for him that the infirmity should remain; for thus would he be kept in closer reliance on the strength which is made perfect in weakness. What we regard as a spiritual blessing, and covet accordingly, might not in the end turn out to be what we hoped for. Much less of course might that which we regard and covet as a temporal blessing be a profitable gift to us.

In the feeling that we know not what to pray for as we ought, we must seek direction in our prayer. We must study Christ's form of prayer to find out thence with what petitions it is lawful and desirable for us to come boldly to the Throne of Grace. And since not only correct petitions, but fervour in offering them, is necessary to the acceptance of our prayers, we must earnestly seek the preventing and assisting grace of that Spirit who helpeth our infirmities, and maketh intercession for us with groanings which cannot be uttered. God's Son putting words into our mouth, and God's Spirit adding direction and fervency to those words, we shall not, cannot, pray in vain. The tongue of Christ, the pleading of Christ's Spirit, what can be more acceptable in the ear of our Father which is in heaven?

CHAPTER V

OUR FATHER WHICH ART IN HEAVEN

'When ye pray,' says our Lord, 'say, Our Father which art in heaven.' But surely He does not mean that saying these words is enough. Prayer does not stand in the utterance of articulate sounds. Nor can He mean that the repetition of the words with bare intelligence — with an understanding of their meaning and an attention to it — is enough. The understanding is not the deepest thing in us. It is indeed good and right to pray with the understanding; but the understanding can only be used as an accompaniment, it is not the faculty wherewith we pray. 'I will pray *with the spirit*,' says the Apostle (this is the essential faculty, the exercise of which constitutes prayer), 'and I will pray *with the under-*

standing also' (showing that the understanding, though necessary, is not the thing *most* necessary). What then is the spirit faculty by which we hold communion with God? It must be the faculty which enables us to form an idea or conception of God. 'No man hath seen God at any time'; and therefore this idea or conception cannot possibly be drawn from experience of sight. Though experience may be needed to develop it, it must be implanted in us from without. None will ever enter into any real communion with God without the exercise of this faculty. If the spirit does not pray, if no high conception is formed in our hearts of the Being whom we are about to address, if no yearning towards Him as the author of our existence and the source of all good, is found there, then our prayer degenerates from the true ideal of prayer, as a reasonable service, into a magical incantation, which can never answer any good purpose.

How then should we conceive of God in prayer? What ideas should we form of Him in our inmost spirit? Our Lord answers this question in the first words of His most precious prayer: 'When ye pray, say'; say, not with your mouth only, not with your mind only, but with your spirit, with the deepest thing within you, 'Our Father which art in the heavens.' These words, like all the words of the Lord's Prayer, are exhaustless in their significance.

First, then, we are to conceive of God, when we resort to Him in prayer, as a Father— a Father in heaven, a Father whose character is marred by none of the weaknesses and imperfections which among ourselves too often detract from the beauty of the parental relationship. God is to be thought of as a Father who is ready, for His Son's sake, to blot out all our sins, and to welcome us back to His bosom despite the worst charges which our conscience may bring against us; as a Father who loves us with infinite tenderness, who consults for us with infinite wisdom, and who calls us in infinite power to second the designs of His love and His wisdom. We are to think of Him as too affectionate to deny us anything which it is really good for us to have, and at the same time as too wise to give us what might be useless or mischievous. But then of course the going to God as a Father, from whom all good may be expected, implies faith in Christ's teaching, faith in the teaching of the parable of the Prodigal Son; and in that other teaching of His about the earthly father who would not give a stone to the hungry child who should clamour to him for bread; Christ being the first who put forth this truth of God's Fatherhood, as the ground of our approach to Him.

We cannot indeed say that there was not in heathenism a blind groping after the truth, that man is, by the original constitution of his nature, a son of God. A heathen poet, speaking of God, had said, 'For we are also His offspring.' Moreover, under the Old Covenant Jehovah had condescended to say of the Jewish nation, 'Israel is My son, even My firstborn.' In like manner the doctrine of a future state was augured, surmised, yearned after, before our Lord's appearance, and yet it was reserved for Him to bring life and immortality to light, to rend the veil which shrouded another world, and to exhibit it to us with clearness and certainty. And thus it was with the doctrine of God's Fatherhood. Man had been made originally in God's image; that is to say, in virtue of his natural faculties he was God's child. His reason was a spark of God's light; his affections were an emanation from God's love. Hence, deeply as man has been estranged from God by sin, there has always been an echo (if we may say so) of God's Fatherhood haunting the chambers of his heart. The restoration of the broken alliance has been incoherently sought after; it has been felt to be that which was needed to satisfy and content the human soul. But after thoughts and yearnings to that effect had been vainly working in man's nature for centuries, without practically influencing his character and conduct, Christ came and announced as a certain truth God's Fatherhood, and His intention of building up anew His family in the Second Adam. Our Lord announced Himself as the Head of the new family, calling Himself the Son of Man; not *a* Son of Man, as the Prophets had been termed, but '*the* Son of Man,' the second and better representative of our race. And God is constantly called by the Apostles the Father of our Lord Jesus Christ, and (by our incorporation into Christ) our Father also. From Nature we might augur God to be powerful, wise, beneficent; but we could gather nothing respecting His Fatherhood. The sight of Nature—its stars and its flowers, its clouds and its sunsets, its winds and its lightnings—would rather awe us by its magnificence than attract us by its sweetness. But Christ's revelation assures us that God is our Father—our reconciled Father in Him. And this assurance having been made on the authority of One who came from heaven, our hearts give an echo to the doctrine as being true, which echo is the protest of our nature in behalf of its original relationship to God. It is said of certain birds which have been hatched and reared by a mother not their own, that if by chance they hear their own mother's cry, the instinct of Nature is so strong that they fly towards her. Whether this be fact or fiction, it is a beautiful illustration of the matter in hand. Born in sin as we have all been, and conceived in iniquity, we have as it were been hatched and reared under the wings of the world and the flesh, and belong to an evil brood. But when Christ announces to us that God is our reconciled Father, our original relationship, not to the world and the flesh, but to God, then asserts itself. We run to Him who calls us back to His home and His bosom, and our hearts say, 'Verily, Thou art our Father.' And it is when we go to God with faith in His reconciliation to us, and faith in His Fatherhood, yearning towards Him as His offspring, seeking refuge under His wings from the toils, vexations, and troubles of the world, from our sins, yea and from ourselves, and expecting greater blessings than we can tell or think from His fatherly interest in us,—then it is that we pray with the spirit or highest faculty of our nature; this is to say, as our Lord has instructed us to say, 'Our Father.'

The next words to be considered give us a further insight into the state of mind in which God should be approached — 'Which art in the heavens.' We are not of course so to understand these words as if they meant that the Divine Presence was limited to heaven. 'He fills heaven and earth,' and 'the heaven and heaven of heavens cannot contain Him.' But Holy Scripture speaks of heaven as of a place where God manifests Himself visibly to the myriads of angels who surround His throne. Though place implies to us limitations of space which are not applicable to the Infinite One, still there is revealed something corresponding to our ideas of a place which bears to the rest of the universe a relation similar to that which the heart bears to the body. Life is diffused throughout the whole body; there are the sensibilities of life, and the movements of life, in the extremities as well as in the vital parts. But the heart is the very source and fountain of living energy. The blood, which is the principle of animal life, is propelled by the heart to all parts of the body. When the heart is still, life is extinct. Similarly, the presence of God, which is diffused throughout His whole universe, finds its chief seat and centre in heaven; and as all movement in the body comes ultimately from the heart, so all the movements of Providence in this lower world—the fortunes of individuals no less than the revolutions of government—are the effects here below of God's administration in heaven above. When heaven is represented to us in Holy Scripture it is usually described (rather than defined) under the image of a temple or sanctuary, because the worship of God is perpetually proceeding in it. It is into this temple that our blessed Lord passed upwards on the day of His Ascension; and it is there that He at present executes for us His high priestly ministration, interceding even for the feeblest and most sinful members of His flock. Our Lord called it His Father's house when He told His disciples that there were many mansions in it, that He went to prepare 'a place' for them, and would return one day to receive them to 'the place' so prepared.

Now to say in our hearts, when we pray, 'Which art in Heaven,' is to approach God with reverence and godly fear. The appellation 'our Father' needs some qualification of this kind. It encourages an affectionate dealing with God as the lover of our souls, as longing to embrace us with the arms of His mercy, as bound to us by ties which even our own undutifulness cannot sunder. But there is another element of feeling which should also pervade our souls when we approach the Throne of Grace. It is that of deepest awe, and profound veneration. No exultation in our religious privileges, no appreciation of God's love, however vivid, should be allowed to expel this graver sentiment of deep awe and profound veneration. The seraphim veil their faces and their feet with their wings when they worship God. And we, the heirs of sinful flesh and blood—not creatures only (like the seraphim), but fallen creatures—shall we not much rather 'rejoice with trembling,' even in our glorious privilege of access to the Majesty on high? And the method of doing this is to realize God as being in the heavens, when we pray; to bear in mind continually the heavenly hierarchy adoring round His throne, and our great High Priest waiting to receive our prayers, and to mingle with them the sweet incense of His intercession. Awe is an essential element of all acceptable worship.

But there is another and equally important thought suggested by the words, 'which art in the heavens.' Couple with these the preceding words 'Our Father,' and the thought immediately arises that heaven is our home. For a father's house, what else is it but a home to the children? If our father is domiciled anywhere, is anywhere specially present, that place, wherever it be, must be our home. And the Christian who says in his heart, 'which art in the heavens,' looks forward to this home in the anticipation of hope, sighs for it, pants after it as the hart after the water-brooks. Here is our encouragement to go to God in a spirit of sanguine hope that, all difficulties and opposition notwithstanding, we shall be brought hereafter to the habitation of His holiness and His glory.

We are privileged to cast behind us the incumbrances of our corrupt nature, to seek God in a bright spirit, a spirit radiant with the hope of glory. Just in proportion to the firmness of our faith will be the liveliness of our hope. In proportion as we grasp firmly the present blessings of forgiveness, acceptance, and peace through the blood of Christ, we shall rejoice keenly in the anticipation of our future recompense. And if hope be dead in our hearts, there is great reason to apprehend that our faith is not a living faith, that it is no more than the acceptance of orthodox doctrine, or at best that it is imagination doing duty for faith.

But before we leave this part of the invocation, it is worthy of notice that here the word heaven is in the plural—'Our Father which art in the heavens,' whereas lower down the word is in the singular, 'Thy will be done in earth, as it is in heaven.' In a composition so studied as the Lord's Prayer, this change of the number is not likely to have been accidental. What then may we suppose it to import? Where angelic obedience and angelic zeal are spoken of, there the singular 'heaven' is used, as being the residence of the holy angels, and so conceived of by Christians. But where man aspires towards his heavenly Father, it is important for him to be reminded that that Father is not far removed from him, but condescends to take up His dwelling in the lowly heart; that there is a spiritual heaven in the heart of believers, as well as a local heaven beyond the stars. This is the doctrine taught by God Himself in the book of the Prophet Isaiah (lvii. 15): 'Thus saith the high and lofty One that inhabiteth eternity, whose name is Holy; I dwell in the high and holy place' (i.e. heaven in the ordinary acceptation of the word), 'with him also that is of a contrite and humble spirit.' Now Heaven being nothing else than God's abode, God's dwelling in any place makes that place heaven. Every humble and contrite believer then, every one who prays in the spirit of the publican in the parable, 'God be merciful to me a sinner,' may and should feel that God is not far from him; that He is nearer than any material object can be; that his heart is a shrine, a heaven, and that God is enthroned there. So that in the term 'which art in the heavens' we find consolation as well as awe.

We have still to consider the word 'our,' and what it teaches as to the spirit in which we should approach God. As then by the word 'Father' we express our faith, and by the words 'which art in Heaven' our hope; so by the word 'our,' or as it is literally 'of us' (and the literal rendering gives more point to the sentiment), we express our connexion, our sympathy, with the whole Church, and our desire to assist (according to our ability) every member of it.

And this sympathy with the whole Church has two sides—a side of obligation and a side of encouragement. Look at it first under the aspect of obligation. It is surely one main reason of unsuccessfulness in prayer that petitions come before God saturated with the deadly tincture of selfishness. Thought of others, interest in others, too rarely enters into our prayers, even though one or two petitions may be appended to them in which we ask His blessing on our friends. And possibly it may seem that to go beyond the narrow circle of those we know and love, to extend our prayer to the Church of Christ, to our nation and its rulers, and to all classes of society, chills the spirit of prayer and deprives it of reality and life. And thus much no doubt is true, that, where there is no sympathy and interest at the bottom of the heart, there can be no real prayer. Prayer for another is the expression of concern for him; and if we have no concern for him, we cannot pray for him. But the Lord's Prayer teaches us most emphatically that this want of concern for our neighbour is a defect which vitiates our prayers; a defect which must be striven against, prayed against, gradually eradicated. Our Lord has so constructed His model Prayer that we cannot pray for ourselves (in language of His dictation) without praying for others. We are God's children because we are members of Christ. And if members of Christ, then members one of another. He has made it impossible for us to recognize the paternal, without at the same time recognizing the fraternal relationship. And His Apostle teaches us that the latter of these relationships is so bound up in the former, that to affect to recognize God as our Father without recognizing men as our brethren is mere hypocrisy: 'If a man say, I love God, and hateth his brother, he is a liar: for he that loveth not his brother, whom he hath seen, how can he love God, whom he hath not seen?'

Then let us seek for and cultivate wider sympathies when we pray. Let us pause momentarily to give a thought to the wants, the sorrows, the sins of our brethren, as well as to our own. Let us fasten the mind (for this will be a help) on any particular burden, under which we know any particular soul to be labouring, and ask for that soul relief—grace, mercy, and peace. It is no strange idea, or one which we find any difficulty in receiving, that we may help others by our alms, or by some definite effort to benefit them temporally. Why should it be strange that we may help them by our prayers?

Moreover, let us look at sympathy with the whole Church in prayer, on its side of encouragement. There is in our own individual prayers a felt weakness and insufficiency which is very disheartening. They are such poor, tame, lifeless things, that our hearts misgive as to their ever finding the way to heaven. Consider, then, that wheresoever and at whatsoever hour thou prayest, thou never prayest alone. Hundreds of cries are rising from other hearts in all parts of the Universal Church. In the stillness and solitude of the night season, no less than in the stir of the day, prayer is being offered by some Christians somewhere. The 'Our Father' may be viewed as the shape in which the prayers of the entire Church reach the ear of God, for what are thousands of '*my* Fathers,' when collected into one comprehensive invocation, and offered for us all in common by our great High Priest, but one '*Our* Father'? It is as if a great cloud of incense were always going up to heaven from every corner of the earth—the incense of holy affections and devout aspirations, kindled upon the heart's altar by the Holy Spirit; or as if, when each of us prayed, even in the solitude of the closet, we brought out our own little censer, and kindled incense there, and added our thin and imperceptible vapour to the great fragrant cloud. The other human souls, which are praying with us and around us, are indeed unconscious of our contribution to their worship. Not so our Divine-Human Priest, who marks from heaven the struggles of each soul after God, and who collects and offers before the throne the suffrages of us all:—

> 'He sees my wants, allays my fears,
> And counts and treasures up my tears.'

From Him we have always *conscious* sympathy. From others we can only look for unconscious co-operation.

We see, then, how much the saying of these first words of the Lord's Prayer implies in the minds of those who use them; how much of faith, of reverence, of hope, of love to God and man. If the Prayer be said in the entire absence of these sentiments, this is no saying it in the ears of God. Nor can any prayer, however excellent the terms in which it is couched, be counted by Him as prayer, unless it be in some measure animated by these sentiments. Words by themselves are nothing. Affections go for everything with Him who is a Spirit, and who will be worshipped in spirit and in truth. If you should whisper but one petition in God's ear, and yet whisper it with faith in His mercy, with yearning after His favour, with sympathy towards His other children, with reference to His Majesty, or with but one of these sentiments working in thy heart—that is prayer. Whereas if thou shouldst recite a whole Liturgy before Him—a Liturgy admirably composed and exhaustive of all the subjects of prayer, and shouldst do so with no opening of the heart either towards God or man, this is no prayer. The voice of the heart—not of the lips, nor even of the mind—is the essence of prayer. Let the heart say but 'Our Father which art in Heaven,' He shall respond to the appeal, and give His blessing, and make us conscious that He gives it.

CHAPTER VI

HALLOWED BE THY NAME

There are seven days in the week. The first of them, the crown and flower of all, belongs in an especial manner to God. The rest belong to man, for the work of his hands and the supply of his daily wants thereby. Similarly, there are seven petitions in the Lord's Prayer. The first of them, the crown and flower of all, is especially directed to God's glory. In the others man's necessities, whether spiritual or bodily, come gradually into view. For even in the two remaining petitions of the first section of the Prayer, the earth and its inhabitants are implied. God's kingdom, for whose coming we pray, is set up upon earth. And His will we pray may be done in earth. But 'Hallowed be Thy name' suggests no thought but of His glory.

This is one of Bishop Andrewes' reflections, though not expressed in his language. And we may carry it a little further. As the Sunday is designed to give a colouring to the days of the week, on all of which it should shed its sanctifying influence, so this petition, standing in the foremost place, colours the meaning of all the other petitions; they would not mean what they do, if they were torn away from their connexion with it.

'Hallowed be Thy name.' What is meant by God's name? and what is meant by hallowing it?

(1) Now we may say generally (it is a simple remark, but not therefore a shallow one) that God's name means very much the same thing as a man's name,—that is to say, his character and reputation, the prevailing impressions about him. We consider a fair fame the greatest of all treasures, and would not barter it away for anything the world can give. What would it profit us to be surrounded by comforts and luxuries, and to live in the possession of everything which wealth can furnish, if every one held a bad opinion of us, distrusted and sus-

pected us, and shunned contact with us? By him who was at once the wisest and the richest of all sovereigns it was said: 'A good name is rather to be chosen than great riches, and loving favour rather than silver and gold.' Now we are told that man was made in the image of God; and accordingly we find that as man sets great store by his good name, so God doth by His, and therefore teaches us to pray that His name may be held in due esteem, before all other petitions whatsoever, even before that for the coming of His kingdom. What would the enlargement of his dominions be to an earthly prince, in comparison of a loyal esteem and devotion to his sacred person in the hearts of his subjects?

But the name of God extends to persons and things which are not strictly part of His character. If a man is held in high esteem and veneration, and has won for himself a universal renown, his children and grandchildren, who carry down his name to posterity, are respected for his sake; and great store is set by any little thing which belonged to him, or which he happened to use, and which after his death may have come into the possession of the others. Thus God's name stands not only for God's reputed character, but for every person and thing associated with Him and bearing memories of Him—for anointed sovereigns, who are His representatives; for ordained ministers, who are His ambassadors; for the Holy Scriptures, which are His word; for the Sunday, which is His day; for the Church, which is His house of prayer; for the bodies of Christians, which are the temples of the Holy Ghost.

But it may be said, ' There are very many traits of God's character mentioned in Holy Scripture; He is called mighty, terrible, true, gracious, merciful, longsuffering, one that will by no means clear the guilty, and by many other names besides. Which, then, of all the Scriptural representations of Him is here particularly meant by His name?' The answer is, that the Divine name embraces of course every attribute ascribed to God in Holy Scripture; but that the character of God, which our blessed Lord both inculcated and exhibited, according to that profound word of His, 'I have manifested Thy name unto the men which

Thou gavest Me,' &c., is the character principally intended here. And it is thus we trace a living connexion between the invocation of the Lord's Prayer and its first petition. The name of God, for the hallowing of which we pray, is the name of 'our Father which is in heaven,' the heavenly Father's name which we adore, and which we have already invoked. That God should be thought of, regarded, esteemed, dealt with by all as a 'Father which is in heaven'; that His parental affection, awful majesty, and eternal distinctness from the creature, should be embalmed and enshrined in all hearts,—this would be some fulfilment of the petition, 'Hallowed be Thy name.'

But what, secondly, is the meaning of the word 'hallowed'? We are in danger of using vaguely this and other words of frequent recurrence in the Scriptures, without ever defining to ourselves what we mean by them. To be hallowed means either to be made holy (a meaning which here the context shows us that it cannot bear; for God's character cannot be made any holier than it is), or to be exhibited, conceived of, and treated, as holy. And this throws us back upon the meaning of the word 'holy'—or rather of the Hebrew word which is so translated—a question of some little difficulty if we sift it to the bottom. The learned are not of one mind as to the radical or fundamental meaning of the word in question. Some suppose the radical meaning to be that of separation; according to which a 'holy' thing would be a thing separated or set apart for sacred uses. Others think that purity or cleanness is the ground-meaning of the word, and that the divers washings prescribed by the Hebrew ritual were designed to initiate the Jews into the idea of holiness, which in its highest application is moral purity. In the application of the word to God we may combine the two ideas, and say that when God is spoken of as holy, it is meant that He is separated by a deep distinction from His creatures, and not to be confounded with them, or they with Him (a sin which is committed in all forms of idolatry); and, secondly, that He is perfectly pure, exempt from all moral obliquity.

As to the Greek or New Testament word which stands for our 'holy,' it comes from a verb which is represented as nearly as possible in our language by 'to venerate, to regard with religious awe.'

On the whole, 'May Thy character, O God, be deeply venerated,' is for all practical purposes a sufficiently accurate paraphrase of the petition, 'Hallowed be Thy name.'

But the idea conveyed by the word 'hallowed' admits of being chiselled a little more, and brought out more sharply. Had our Saviour instructed us to pray, as He might have done, 'Glorified be Thy name,' would there have been any difference in the meaning? Yes, certainly. To glorify God's name is not quite the same thing as to hallow it. Irrational and inanimate creatures may glorify God's name; but only moral agents can hallow it. Every flower by its fair hues, every leaf by its delicate tracery of veins and its tender green, every insect by its wonderful structure, every star by its radiance, glorifies God, declares, that is, His glory and His magnificence. And accordingly the Psalmist sings, 'The heavens declare the glory of God.'

The whole realm of Nature is a mirror which reflects the glory of the Creator, His skill, His power, His magnificence, His grandeur. But the mirror in which God's holiness is reflected is the hearts and souls of His rational creatures. These hearts and souls venerate, adore Him, lie low before Him in conscious homage; yea, more than this, God's moral image is by grace reproduced in them;—'the new man,' says St. Paul, 'is renewed in knowledge after the image of Him that created him.' The petition, therefore, 'Hallowed be Thy name,' if at all deeply considered, involves the idea of rational moral agents, whether men or angels, by whom and among whom it may be 'hallowed.'

And though it may well be said that God's character is not really known to us; that as yet we know not as we are known; that the Infinite God must necessarily be beyond the contemplation of a finite mind; that 'no man hath seen God'— seen Him with the mind's eye—'at any time'; that God, fixedly looked upon, dazzles and bewilders the human reason, even as the sun, fixedly looked upon, dazzles and disables the bodily eye. 'But the Only-begotten Son, which is in the bosom of the Father, He hath declared Him.' 'He that hath seen Jesus hath seen the Father'; and we have no need thenceforward to say, 'Show us the Father.' The character of Christ is the character of God reflected in the mirror of a sinless humanity. God's tender yearning over the worst sinners, His infinite compassion for, and condescension to, the infirmities of man, His deep abhorrence of insincerity and untruth, His strict and sensitive purity, His piercing insight into the most hidden things of human character, His sifting dealings with the consciences of individuals, His vast power, never displayed for its own sake, but always to subserve some beneficent end, His wonderful forbearance towards those who provoke and defy Him,—all these traits shine forth luminously in the career of our Lord Jesus Christ. And the great complex of them forms a character irresistibly attractive to simple and sincere souls. This was the spell which drew the disciples to

Him; not the mere sight of His miracles, though that of course confirmed the impression, but the beauty of holiness which streamed through His whole life and conversation, the sweetness and majesty of His demeanour, which was a true exhibition of God in the flesh.

The significance of the position of this petition in the prayer is great. 'Hallowed be Thy name' stands before all other petitions—and why? (1) to teach us a lesson as to prayer; (2) a lesson as to piety; (3) a lesson as to the supreme object of human desire.

And, first, a lesson as to prayer. This petition stands first by way of teaching us that the homage which we pay to God in prayer is the first and principal thing in it, and necessary to win Him to comply with our petitions. There are two aspects of prayer, totally distinct, and yet closely interwoven with one another. One is, that prayer is a means of supplying human necessities, whether spiritual or temporal. Another is, that prayer is an acknowledgment of Almighty God, an homage done to His perfections. Under the first of these aspects, prayer is like standing in a crowd, to see a sovereign pass, and throwing a petition at his feet. Under the second of these aspects, prayer is like resorting to the Court, simply to pay one's homage, without any ulterior object. Now by placing this petition first, our blessed Lord teaches that the second of these aspects of prayer is the more important and the more vital of the two. We must adore God in the inner man, before we venture to present any petitions to Him. It is much to have appeared before Him in His heavenly court, to have bowed the knee of the heart before Him, and to have joined our feeble 'Hallowed be Thy name' to the seraphim's thrice repeated cry of 'Holy, Holy, Holy,' even if we carry away nothing from the Throne of Grace. For prayer is primarily a duty of loyalty. Only in its lower character is it a means of supplying human needs. My reader, have you sufficiently considered in your practice the higher aspect of prayer? Do you go to God merely for what you can get, or do you go also to pay homage? Is your prayer nothing more than an asking? or is it a worship?

And even where petition forms the great burden of the strain, are you careful before you begin, to excite in your heart by every means in your power emotions of reverence and awe towards the great Being before whom you prostrate yourself?

Secondly, we learn from the circumstance of this petition's standing first, a deeply important lesson as to piety. We are taught by this circumstance that a right apprehension of God's character lies at the root of all true piety, and that where there is a wrong apprehension of that character, there piety is corrupted at its spring. By a law from whose operation none of us can escape, the worshipper becomes unconsciously assimilated to the object of his worship. This law has been exemplified a thousand times in the history of false religions. And the ground of it is not difficult to discern. The character of our God will be with all of us the ideal standard of perfection, to which we shall seek (consciously or unconsciously) to conform ourselves. Our views of God cannot but insensibly shape our character and conduct; in vain shall we strive to resist the influence of those views, or to establish a religiousness which shall be independent of them; we might as well strive to withdraw the tides from the constant influence of the moon's attraction. 'All people,' says the Prophet Micah, 'will walk every one in the name of His God'; will conduct himself, that is, according to the conceived character of the God with whom he has to do; 'and we will walk,' adds he, 'in the name of the Lord our God for ever and ever.'

Now this holy resolution of God's people finds itself embodied in the opening of their daily prayer. For they are instructed to pray before all things else that God's name may be hallowed in their hearts, and in the hearts of all around them. Because indeed everything will go well in the spiritual life, where this hallowing takes place; every thing as infallibly will go ill, where the name of God is degraded, thought lightly of, regarded with slavish terror, or with presumption, or with indifference.

One of the best tests then of personal piety which can be applied to ourselves, a better and more stringent test by far than any amount of religious exercise or devout observance, is wrapped up in the question, 'What think ye of God?' Is God merely a law of Nature with you (He is practically so to many), the influence which keeps the system of the universe at work, but having no free-will, manifesting no spontaneous emotion, no moral choice—God stripped of that which constitutes the nobility of man—individual personality? Is there an element of the divine in everything, as some prate, in flowers, in stars, in sunsets, in landscapes, in clouds, in the sea, in men, in natural affection, in natural intellect, in natural enthusiasm, in a mother's love, in a nation's patriotism—and beyond the beautiful in all these things, is there no God? In short, is God merely the charm of Nature, diffused subtilly through the whole of it, but having, independently of Nature, neither a local habitation nor a name? This is not the God of the Lord's Prayer, for whose name we pray that it may be hallowed, kept i.e. in distinctness and veneration, above every name that is named. This is a God inseparably mixed up with the creature, and having no distinct existence—an idolater's God. Or do you think of God as upon the whole liable to be lax in His judgement upon sin, as threatening it with frightful punishments which He has too much clemency to inflict, as readily tolerating in us all certain stains and specks of sin, so long as they are not very black and very flagrant? Is He one who will readily accept us, if we are only on a par with our neighbours in point of moral and religious attainment? This again is not the God of the Lord's Prayer, for whose name we pray that it may be hallowed—deeply venerated in men's hearts, held to be of stainless purity, and eternally exempt from all complicity with sin. Or, again, do you entertain a severe notion of God? Is His service thought of as a series of irksome restrictions, 'touch not, taste not, handle not'? Do we dread a close contact with Him, desire to keep Him at arm's length, turn our backs upon that ordinance in which He comes into the most immediate neighbourhood with us? Alas! this is not the God of the Lord's Prayer, whose name is 'Our Father which art in heaven,' and the hallowing of whose name principally stands in the conception of Him as abounding in parental love.

But in order to give a further point and definiteness to this test, let us change the form of the question, and, since Christ is the image of the invisible God, let us ask in the very words of the Saviour, 'What think ye of Christ?' We can all form a sufficient idea of His character and deportment, of His ways and words, as reported by the holy Evangelists. We read of His infinite condescension to the humblest, of His deep sympathy with the afflicted, of His patient sweetness with the perverse, of His plain dealing with all consciences, of His withering denunciations of hypocrites, of His lofty standard of precept, far above the moral requirements of the Mosaic Law—the standard of absolute purity and invincible love. Well, is this attractive to us? should we have been drawn by it into the charmed circle of His followers, not, as Judas was drawn, by the prospect of an earthly kingdom in which He would make us sharers? or rather, as we may believe Peter, and John, and Mary, and Martha, were all more or less drawn by the strange fascination of His character, the unearthly beauty of His way of life? Or should we have stood outside with the world of that day, sneering, carping, misrepresenting, reviling? endeavouring as far as in us lay to suppress Him and His work altogether? It is a solemn question for each one of us, and not to be settled hastily. But by it we may ascertain how far we are hallowing God's name. For the character of Christ is God's character mirrored in humanity. And therefore to venerate Christ profoundly, and to feel in truth and sincerity the full attractiveness and power of His character, is to hallow God's character and render to Him the homage which is His due.

But, lastly, we learn from the position of the petition before us a lesson as to the supreme object of human desire and human endeavour. For beyond all doubt the petition which stands first must indicate by its precedence what should be the fondest wish of the human heart. What is prayer but a wish finding utterance before God in words? The first prayer therefore which Christ puts into our lips must needs represent what should be our strongest desire. Here then is another test to apply to our consciences; for what a test are our desires of our moral and spiritual state! Are they not *the* test—the test by the application of which our moral and spiritual condition may be most readily and most immediately ascertained? We read that 'the Lord appeared to Solomon in a dream by night: and God said, Ask what I shall give thee' (1 Kings iii. 5). The question was designed to be a test of Solomon's character, and of his fitness to meet the heavy responsibilities and grapple with the arduous duties which the inheritance of the throne of David brought with it. Solomon, feeling himself to be sadly unfit for these duties and responsibilities, asked for the wisdom which might qualify him for his position—in other words, which have to our ears a very familiar ring, he asked for grace 'to do his duty in that state of life unto which it had pleased God to call him.' Suppose now the same offer were made to us as to Solomon, what good thing out of all God's treasury would our hearts, lying naked and open under the eye of God's omniscience, prompt us to choose? That God's will, whatever it be, should be done in us, by us, upon us—would this be the supreme desire? Happy man, or woman, who can say so sincerely;—yet not the happiest! Or would it be that God's influence should be far more widely spread among men, than it is, that the home mission, that the foreign mission should become mighty forces in the world, tending daily more and more to the extension and establishment of God's kingdom? *Twice* happy man, or woman, who can say so sincerely;—yet not the happiest! For there is a thing which lies closer to God's heart, closer (if I may venture to say so) to Himself, than either the doing of His will or the coming of His kingdom. And this is His name—His character, as distinct from the acts of His will, which result from the working of His character, and as distinct from His empire, which results from the exhibition of His character. His name or character is nearer to Him than either His kingdom or His will, lying, as it does, underneath both these. And therefore *thrice* happy is the man, or the woman, who can sincerely say that his supreme wish is that the Lord God should be sanctified in his own heart and in the hearts of all around him—regarded as the Heavenly Father, with unreserved confidence and yearning affection, and yet with deepest awe and reverence, as by those angelic worshippers who veil their faces and their feet with their wings, as they cry one to another, 'Holy, holy, holy, is the Lord God of hosts: the whole earth is full of His glory.'

CHAPTER VII

THY KINGDOM COME

ONE has heard of the perspective of prophecy. It is a great feature of inspired predictions to have a long perspective. By this we mean that the graver prophecies, and those which are of universal concern, are not fulfilled by one single event, but by a series of events standing in some relation to one another, either as types, or as gradual preparatives of the last and consummating fulfilment. Our Lord's great prophecy on the Mount of Olives, after He had taken His leave of the Temple, is an instance in point. He predicts there two great events, the destruction of Jerusalem and the end of the world. There is a real and close connexion between them, inasmuch as the first was the judgement of the Jewish, and the second will be the judgement of the Christian Church. The two events are seen in perspective, like two mountain ranges in front of a spectator, one rising behind the other, and the eye taking no cognizance of the intermediate tract of space, which may be immense. And accordingly the eye of the Divine speaker glances rapidly from summit to summit; and now one of these great events seems to be uppermost in His thoughts, and now another. From this characteristic of inspired prophecy comes a mysterious richness in its predictions. It would be meagre and bald in comparison if it were fulfilled by one historical crisis, and did not involve a perspective.

Now we may speak of a perspective in prayer, as well as of a perspective in prophecy. And the petition before us is an excellent instance (probably the best that could be furnished) of a *long* perspective in prayer. The *final* answer to it will never be given until the second Advent arrives, when the Son of God, having put down all rule, and all authority, and power, shall deliver up the kingdom to

God, even the Father, that God may be all in all. For it is emphatically *God's* kingdom for the coming of which Christ here instructs us to pray. But there are, and will be, many previous answers, all conducing towards this ultimate consummation. The petition before us is answered by any accession to Christ's mediatorial kingdom. It is answered whenever a Jew, a Turk, an infidel, or an heretic, is converted. It is answered again, whenever a merely nominal Christian becomes by God's grace a real one. It is answered, again, whenever a real Christian makes a new spiritual attainment, grows in grace and in the knowledge of our Lord and Saviour Jesus Christ.

Or, to use the very words in which we teach our catechumens, not to be despised, but rather to be valued, on account of their utter simplicity: 'When we say "Thy kingdom come," we pray, first, that all who are not at present Christians may become so; secondly, that all bad Christians may become good ones; thirdly, that all good Christians may become better ones; and, lastly, that the Lord would come again to receive all good Christians unto Himself.' This petition then is being fulfilled continually all over the world. But it will not receive its final fulfilment till the end of time.

There is a kingdom of God which cannot be advanced by human efforts and human prayers; a kingdom which is at present fully established among us, which is here and needs not to come; a kingdom at which we glance in the doxology annexed to this prayer, when we say, 'Thine *is* the kingdom.' God's kingdom of providence ruleth everywhere even now; and we are all, voluntarily or involuntarily, consciously or unconsciously, the subjects of it. All events, however adverse they seem to the Divine plans, all actions of men, however perversely intended by their agents, fall immediately under the control of Him who is Light and Love, and are made subordinate to the great ends of His administration. Great is the comfort to a godly mind of knowing that the kingdom of Divine Providence has the supreme control of all events; and that its great and inviolable law is this: 'All things work together for good to them that love God, to them who are the called according to His purpose.'

But we are now in search of some kingdom of God which is capable of being advanced by human prayer and human effort. The first petition of the Lord's Prayer is on behalf of God's holy character—of Himself; 'Hallowed be Thy name.' In offering that first petition, we view God as He is in Himself, in the intrinsic excellence and beauty of His Divine nature. But in the second petition we view Him in His relation to His creatures, for we speak of His kingdom. Now a kingdom must have subjects; the correlative idea to that of a king is a subject. And looking once again at the petition, we find in it a further implication. It appears that the King, whom we are addressing, must have disobedient and disloyal subjects. For if this were not so, what could be the meaning of a petition that His kingdom might *come*? How could there be any advance in allegiance to Him, if allegiance be universally and perfectly paid at present? And yet if God is indeed almighty, as we believe, how can any creature exist who is not subject to His sway? Here, then, is for the first time developed the great mystery of man's freewill. In the prayer that God's kingdom may come it is intimated that there are agencies which oppose and counteract His kingdom, that there are rational creatures who are not, or are but imperfectly, subject to His control. That these rational creatures may be brought to submit to His control or to acknowledge it more entirely, that these opposing agencies may be successively taken out of the way or overruled, this is the first thing we ask for in the petition before us; this it is which must prepare the way for the ultimate consummation.

But in order to arrive at a clear and methodical apprehension of the whole subject, let us place ourselves in the position of those to whom the Prayer was first given, and consider what kind of answer it has received between their time and the present, how far the fulfilment of it has been developed since it was first put into their lips. Our blessed Lord then opened His ministry by taking up the echoes which had died away upon the lips of John the Baptist: 'Repent ye; for the kingdom of heaven is at hand.' This kingdom of heaven, then, would certainly be the kingdom to which the Apostles would understand Him as referring when He taught them to pray, 'Thy kingdom come.' And being Jews, and intimately acquainted with the Jewish Scriptures, they would as certainly understand this kingdom to be that predicted by the prophet Daniel: 'And in the days of these kings' (Roman Emperors) 'shall the God of heaven set up a kingdom which shall never be destroyed: nor shall the sovereignty thereof be left to another people, but it shall break in pieces and consume all these kingdoms; and it shall stand for ever.' They must further have understood our Lord Himself to lay claim to be King of this kingdom, not in His own right, but as representing God, and being God's delegate and viceroy, as is abundantly clear from the greetings of the whole multitude of the disciples on occasion of the triumphal entry: 'Blessed be the King that cometh in the Name of the Lord: peace in heaven, and glory in the highest.' This kingdom seems to have been the one great subject in which our Lord instructed them. He copiously illustrated its rise and progress by His parables; He pointed to His miracles of exorcism as indicating that the kingdom of God had come upon (overtaken) the men of that generation; even in the forty days which intervened between the Resurrection and the Ascension, this was His constant topic of discourse: 'He spake of the things pertaining to the kingdom of God.' Even so late as that, their views of the nature of the kingdom were dark, carnal, and erroneous; they thought of it mainly as the restoration to the chosen people, under a brighter and more beautiful form, of the monarchy of David, which had been so long in abeyance. But ten days after the Ascension, the kingdom came with power, and brought with it its own interpretation of its nature and prerogatives. The Apostles after Pentecost perceived the kingdom of God to be spiritual, while they perceived it also to involve a certain visible organization, into which men were to be brought, quite independently of blood or extraction. They went forth on their different missions to bring men within the kingdom, by heralding to them God's message respecting the Son of His Love. And when the inspired chronicler of the acts of the Apostles has brought St. Paul (who was born out of due season into the glorious company of the Apostles) to Rome, the centre of civilization, and the then metropolis of the world, he leaves him there with this pregnant notice of the testimony which he bore: 'Paul dwelt two whole years in his own hired house, and received all that came in unto him, preaching the kingdom of God.' And since Paul and the other inspired men fell asleep, the kingdom of God, realizing the similitude of a grain of mustard seed to which its King compared it, has gone on expanding and shooting forth its branches, until, if not a numerical majority of the human race, at all events all the more civilized and influential portion of it has become Christian by profession. One might have anticipated for this kingdom—founded by the Son of God and seconded by His Spirit—a triumphant career, unchecked by any drawbacks, and unqualified by any reverses. But natural as these anticipations might have been on mere grounds of reason, they would have been wholly opposed to prophecy. The King of the kingdom, and those under Him who founded it, predicted most explicitly for it a dark, rather than a bright future. According to the parable of the sower, the word of the kingdom was only to thrive in one out of every four hearts on which it was thrown. So the tares sown by the great Enemy of mankind were to spring up side by side with the wheat in the field of the kingdom. The net of the kingdom was to enclose fish of every kind, both good and bad. A mystery of iniquity was already in St. Paul's time working in the Church, which was to develop itself in awful dimensions, when a certain mysterious hindrance was withdrawn, waxing into a great apostasy and rising to a head in the appearance of one who is designated as 'that man of sin, the son of perdition' (2 Thess. ii. 3). St. Peter warned the Church with failing breath that in the latter days there should be 'scoffers, walking after their own lusts,' and 'false teachers, who privily should bring in damnable heresies; even denying the Lord that bought them' (2 Pet. ii. 1 ; iii. 3). The aged St. John reminded his disciples that Antichrist should come; and that the pledge of his coming was to be found in the fact that his spirit was even then abroad in the world, and that there were many subordinate and preliminary antichrists, who partook of that spirit (1 John iv. 3). So that the picture which both our Lord and His Apostles drew beforehand of the future of the kingdom of God comprised two great features—rapid spread and deep corruption. Both features have been constantly and faithfully exhibited in the history of the Church, and are now under our eyes. On the one hand, the countries which stand in the van of civilization, and represent the chief intellect of mankind, are nominally Christian. The spires and domes of Christian churches form the most characteristic feature of the greatest cities in the world. The greatest sovereigns in the world have taken such titles as 'Defender of the Faith' and 'Most Christian King.' But if the outward spread of God's kingdom has been great, equally great has been the spread of the gangrene of corruption. What a frightful departure from the first principles of the Gospel is manifest and patent on the surface of Christendom! How is the one fold of Christ, whose unity He made the special subject of His dying intercession, broken up and parted off into hundreds of folds! Anti-scriptural doctrines and superstitious practices, worthy only of Paganism, are still fostered in some communions; while our own Church, like Rebecca with the children striving within her, is distracted by errors, on one side Roman, on another Puritan, on another Rationalistic. This glance at the Church's history up to this time gives a very definite meaning to the petition, 'Thy kingdom come.' On the one hand, we pray for the rapid spread of the kingdom, by means of all those agencies, preaching, missions, schools, religious literature, which are instrumental to this end. On the other, we pray no less for the removal of everything which obstructs the development of the kingdom in righteousness; for the extinction of heresies; the suppression of scandals; the reconciliation of schisms; the exhibition by professing Christians of a holy example; the agreement of all those who confess God's holy name in the truth of His holy Word.

And let us offer this prayer hopefully and sanguinely, looking forward with assurance to its ultimate fulfilment. Let us be nothing dismayed by the evils and errors which abound. Let us consider, first, how certain it is that He who originally founded the kingdom in so marvellous a way, by the instrumentality of twelve Galilaean fishermen, and without the aid of arms, eloquence, or power, will surely never suffer so grand and glorious a commencement to be abortive, will rather (as at any instant He might) send a second Pentecost, or raise up a second St. Paul. Secondly, let us note that the large admixture of evil with good seems in this fallen world to be a necessary condition of progress; so that the vices, errors, and schisms, which so disfigure modern Christianity, may after all indicate a real and deep movement of grace in the heart of individuals, and among the masses, which Satan is thus endeavouring to counteract. Lastly, we may take great comfort and gather new hope from remembering that 'the kingdom of God cometh not with observation'; that as to its essence, it consists in nothing outward, but in a certain character and frame of mind, being 'not meat and drink, but righteousness, and peace, and joy in the Holy Ghost'; and that therefore its real progress is unnoticed, while the things which obstruct its development meet the eye and strike upon the ear. The work of grace, by which the kingdom is advanced, is an underground process. Its seat is the conscience which is gradually enlightened, the will which is gradually drawn up into compliance with God's will, the heart which is only gradually and by successive disciplines of Providence weaned from things of earth. Who ever imagined that the seed was killed, because a hard winter encrusted every bough with icicles, and covered the ground with a mantle of snow? The seed is bursting during this inclement season, and disentangling its germ; but the process goes on beneath the soil. By-and-by the tender sprout will rise above the surface; and then will follow the bud, and then the blossom in its season. The ripened fruit is the full and visible result; but it is a result which has been prepared by tedious and hidden agencies. God's kingdom of glory, when it arrives, will be a full and visible result. But it will have been brought about 'without observation,' hiddenly and gradually in the deep ground of the heart.

We now turn to trace the bearings of our subject on Christian practice.

And first as to the kingdom of grace, whose progress we profess to desire in this petition. How does such a petition match with our lives? How far do our actions betoken any sincerity in offering it? God's kingdom is to be advanced not by our prayers only, but by our efforts in combination with our prayers. Then what efforts are we making for its advancement? What are we doing for Christian missions to the heathen abroad?

I fear that in the great majority of cases, while this petition is recited punctually at least twice every day, the corresponding effort to assist foreign missions is not made regularly and systematically at all,—in short is never made, except when the subject is brought before us by the annual sermon. And in other cases, where the yearly guinea, the loss of which is never felt, is duly given, and so the duty recognized, is it given with any amount of sympathy or interest in the cause? Do we care at all how God's work is progressing among the heathen? Have we ever taken the pains to inform ourselves about its progress?

But there are heathens in our own country, who, it will be admitted on all hands, have a prior claim upon us—souls numbered by thousands in our large towns, the refuse of our high civilization, who from one year's end to another never attend a place of public worship, who know not whether they have ever been baptized, whose whole notions on religious subjects, if they were not in a high degree painful and shocking, would be in a high degree grotesque. Many efforts are being made to bring in these multitudes into the kingdom. Do we feel, and do we evince, any sympathy with these efforts? Do we aid them according to our abilities and opportunities?

If in examining our hearts narrowly, we find at the bottom of them very little interest and sympathy with the Christianization of others, whether at home or abroad, what a hollow mockery is it to recite before God several times a day a prayer, whose very structure and purport implies that we desire before daily bread—before meat and drink and raiment—the extension of His kingdom upon earth. False pretences are too common in all our prayers. But in no other prayer is so much false pretence liable to be habitually made as in the Lord's Prayer; first because the standard of piety supposed in the petitioner is so high, and secondly because the use of the prayer is so universal. On the lips of the majority of Christians this holy and beautiful form is merely lip-service. Even in days like these, when religious education is so widely spread, the vast majority of Christians in reciting it never realize what it implies; or they would shrink from the notion of offering to the heart-searching God a petition the insincerity of which, as preferred by them, He must immediately detect.

But it is in respect of the ulterior meaning of the words, 'Thy kingdom come,' that the insincerity, with which they are so frequently uttered, assumes its most awful aspect. For, as we have seen, the consummation for which we here pray, the great event which is the point of sight in the long perspective of the kingdom of grace, to which every line of that kingdom converges, is the second Advent of our Lord. The petition is a prayer for the second Advent, as well as for the acceleration of those preparatory processes by which the second Advent is to be brought about. And we present it to God in an expanded form, when, standing over the grave of some dear relative and friend, we join mentally in the request, 'We beseech Thee that it may please

Thee of Thy gracious goodness shortly to accomplish the number of Thine elect, and to *hasten Thy kingdom.*' But if our life be a careless and a worldly one; if we never make up our spiritual accounts and see how they stand; if we never turn our eyes upon Christ's judgement-seat, nor prepare ourselves to meet Him when He sits upon it; if, moreover, we have no heart for that heavenly kingdom of God which His advent will usher in, no relish for that righteousness and peace and joy which will universally prevail in the new heavens and new earth; if in short there is in us at present no meetness for the kingdom of glory,—then the petition to hasten this kingdom is nothing more nor less than calling down judgement upon ourselves, and asking God to shorten the term during which His longsuffering waits to lead us to repentance. Some indeed of the worldly-minded do this from mere thoughtlessness and undesignedly, but there are, alas! others who have more of method and meaning in their madness. The history of many a suicide is this, that a man's worldly prospects being broken, his fortunes, his character, or his constitution (or perhaps all three) having received a fatal blight, a heathenish sentiment comes flitting across his mind that in the grave peace and exemption from cares and suffering may be found, independently altogether of character and conduct here below. And so he rushes upon death prematurely, forestalling to himself by his own wilful and wicked action the coming of the kingdom. And what is the kingdom to him, when it does come? Alas! an infinitely more dreadful evil than any of which while living he had experience. Where he fancied he should find a haven of refuge, he finds a stormy sea of wrath and the shipwreck of his soul. What he hoped would prove a home to him proves in fact the condition of an outcast; as it was said of old by the prophet Amos, with a very lively and striking imagery: 'Woe unto you that desire the day of the Lord! to what end is it for you? the day of the Lord is darkness, and not light. As if a man did flee from a lion, and a bear met him; or went into his house, and leaned his hand on the wall, and a serpent bit him.'

Then let us never dare to make such a prayer as this without seeking in penitence something of that righteousness and peace and joy in the Holy Ghost which constitute the meetness for the inheritance of the saints in light. Let us have humble but sure ground for thinking that God's kingdom, should it come to us to-night, would indeed bring to us exemption from all sorrows, and wipe away all tears from our faces. So and so only, we shall be in harmony with God's whole universe. For it is for this blessed consummation that all the creatures, and we may be sure the spirits of the righteous dead, yearn and long, even as it is written: 'The earnest expectation of the creature waiteth for the manifestation of the sons of God. For the creature was made subject to vanity, not willingly, but by reason of Him who hath subjected the same in hope; because the creature itself also shall be delivered from the bondage of corruption into the glorious liberty of the children of God.

For we know that the whole creation groaneth and travaileth in pain together until now. And not only they, but ourselves also, which have the firstfruits of the Spirit, even we ourselves groan within ourselves, waiting for the adoption, to wit, the redemption of our body.'

CHAPTER VIII

THY WILL BE DONE

In most of the subjects of human knowledge the rudiments may be dispensed with as soon as the subject has been thoroughly mastered. Grammars and exercise books may be thrown away when a language has been duly acquired; and the man who can read fluently never turns again to his alphabet or spelling-book. But it is otherwise in theology, which is the highest study of all, and the highest subject of knowledge. Here the rudiments, in which children are instructed, contain the deepest parts of the science; and however advanced a Christian may be in the knowledge of God's Word, and in experimental acquaintance with Divine truth, he will always return with pleasure and profit to the Lord's Prayer, the Creed, and the Ten Commandments;

especially to the first of these, and find there new treasures of edification, and new depths which he has not yet explored. The structure of other sciences resembles that of a house, which is built by placing the materials in successive layers one upon another. The Divine science of theology, on the other hand, is like a seed, which contains in itself the germ of the flower. Learning in the one case is only an agglomeration of fresh materials to those already laid; learning in the other case is the expansion and development of old and well-known truths.

The petitioner has just sent up to heaven sighs and prayers that the kingdom of God may come, that is, for the arrival of the kingdom of glory by the extension and acceleration of the kingdom of grace. Now he bethinks himself that he must add active endeavours to his adoration and his aspirations, according to that word of the Divine Master, 'Not every one that saith unto Me, Lord, Lord, shall enter into the kingdom of heaven; but he that doeth the will of My Father which is in heaven.'

We have been hitherto like the Apostles at the Ascension, looking wistfully upwards into heaven and adoring our ascended Lord; but now we seem to hear the trumpet-tones of the two men in white garments, suggesting His return as the necessary goal of their thoughts and expectations and energies: 'Ye men of Galilee, why stand ye gazing up into heaven? This same Jesus, who is taken up from you into heaven, shall so come in like manner as ye have seen Him go into heaven.'

'Thy will be done.' Let us endeavour to see what view of God is now introduced into the Prayer. In the first petition we regarded God as having a name or character; 'Hallowed be Thy name.' In the second we regarded Him as having subjects who might, or might not, do allegiance to Him and be obedient to His sceptre. In the third we regard Him as having a will of His own; 'Thy will be done.'

Here then is brought prominently forward what of course has been previously implied—nay, what is implied in the mere fact of prayer at all—the doctrine of God's personality. In speaking of God's kingdom, and looking around us on the realm of Nature, we might imagine perchance that we are under the empire of pure law. For what we see in Nature is a number of laws, working ruthlessly on with mechanical precision, never turning aside for an instant, nor altering their course for friend or foe. And it is easy to imagine—for indeed the pantheist does imagine—that we are in the hand of law; that God, or the ruling power in Nature, is a law or a series of laws—an influence which is ever manifesting itself in different forms in the various phenomena of the universe, and which is not even conscious of itself. God, according to the pantheist, is that subtle, impalpable, universal life, which blooms in the flower, which glows in the star, which sparkles on the face of the sunlit deep, which imagines in the poet, which argues in the orator, which aspires in the devout.

To say that these various manifestations of life in Nature are from God and that they are sustained by His power is of course true; for 'in Him we live, and move, and have our being.'

But to confound them with Him, and to turn

universal Nature into God, is to become an idolater. All such fooleries of sentiment are swept away at once by the assertion that God has a will. A will is that which characterizes a person. A mere influence has no will. A law, which unconsciously works itself out, and which has no choice but to work itself out, has no will. But we acknowledge in this Prayer that God has a will; and we pray that His will may have place or take effect. God therefore is a Person, and we are to think of Him as such.

But what is meant, in strictness of speech, by a will? Will is the faculty of rational choice. The lower animals have the semblance of will, inasmuch as in their natural state they are free to go hither and thither, free to eat, drink, and sleep, or to refrain from these actions; but this is not rational choice, because in what they do, or refrain from doing, they are simply actuated by the impulse of the moment. If they were capable (as to all appearance they are not) of preferring a future good to a present gratification, and of acting accordingly, they would be possessed of will; for in this case, from being merely appetitive, their choice would become rational. In order to make a choice rational, there must be foresight and power of forecasting in the person making the choice, and also the moral faculty of discriminating right from wrong.

Now this definition will forward our subject considerably. For we are now considering God's will; and what has been said leads us naturally to observe upon the great distinction between will as it is in God, and will as it is in fallen man. What is called will in man is oftentimes nothing better than caprice. It is not rational or moral choice, although exercised by a creature having the faculty of rational or moral choice. It is a mere whim, of which no account, or no reasonable account, can be given. Our attraction to one man more than another, our preference of one man over another, is often due to no other assignable cause than fancy. But this is an infirmity of the will—a manifest defect, which we must not for an instant imagine to exist in the all-perfect and blessed God. Hooker somewhere calls attention to the circumstance that even when the Apostle Paul is speaking of God's predestination, he guards against being supposed to imply that in this mysterious procedure God acts arbitrarily and without grounds in reason. 'Being predestinated according to the purpose of Him who worketh all things,' (not after His own will, but) 'after the counsel of His own will.' So that even in that act of God which might seem arbitrary, because we cannot fathom the reason of it, there yet is a reason, a deep counsel, a wise thought. God forbid that we should think (for such a thought really entertained would poison the fountain of piety) that in His acceptance of one man and rejection of another He is actuated by caprice; although indeed some people do not hesitate to imply this, when they prate about God's sovereignty.

One more remark must be made upon this petition, before leaving the speculative part of the subject. The Lord's Prayer being a fabric wonderfully joined together and compacted by that which every joint supplieth, we shall in vain seek to understand it, we shall certainly go astray in it, unless we take into account the relation which its several parts bear to one another. The first petition, 'Hallowed be Thy name,' is not accidentally the first; it is the keynote which pervades and dominates the strain. It gives a character to the whole Prayer; it throws a colour on to the succeeding petitions. Thus with 'Thy kingdom come.' What sort of kingdom is God's? Men have set up kingdoms and empires many, and have brought people into them by force. Such was Caesar's kingdom. If provinces were rebellious or discontented, a conquering legion swept over them, and the rebellion or the murmur subsided in the awful Pax Romana. Is God's kingdom of this sort? or is this the way in which it is to be made to come or maintained afterwards. Assuredly not. Where is the keynote which is to rule the melody of the prayer? Here it is; 'Hallowed be Thy name;'—may Thy character, O God, be universally acknowledged and have universal homage paid to it! But what is God's true character? We will learn it from His own Word. There we find two brief but pregnant oracles to this effect; 'God is light' and 'God is love.' 'Light,' that is, if I may so say, the great complex of the intellectual attributes; love, that is the great complex of His moral attributes. Well then, I am to understand God's kingdom as being a kingdom in accordance with His character, a kingdom of light and a kingdom of love. And if it be a kingdom of light and love, it cannot come or be established by physical force; its coming must be in the convictions of the conscience, in the dawning of truth upon the mind, in the wider diffusion of a practical and experimental knowledge of God, and of holy tempers flowing from that experimental knowledge. The kingdom is to be interpreted by the name of Him whose kingdom it is. And so with regard to the will. Here too the petition is to take its interpretation from what went before. If 'Thy will be done' were an isolated petition; if it grew not naturally out of what precedes it in the prayer; we might imagine that God's will was an arbitrary one, subject to infirmities of caprice and partiality like our own. But observe that God's will must be in accordance with His name, which is light and love. As the kingdom of One whose name is light and love cannot possibly be a kingdom of physical force, must be a kingdom of intelligence and sympathy, standing on the convictions and affections of men; so the will of One whose name is light and love cannot possibly be a groundless, arbitrary, partial, or exclusive will—must be grounded in wise counsel, however hidden from us that counsel may be; and must intend good, the highest good, and nothing but good, to the whole race of man and to each individual member of it.

And now, by way of resolving our petition into its main ideas, we will take, as we did before, the words in which our catechumens are taught, and say that the will of God, for which we here pray that it may take place or have effect, is (so far as we are interested in it) either a will concerning us, or a will within us, or a will to be executed by us. According as we view the petition in these several aspects, it will be either the voice of resignation, 'Thy will be done in what befalls me'; or the voice of dependence, 'Work in me, O God, both to will and to do of Thy good pleasure'; or the voice of holy energy, 'Make me Thy instrument for the fulfilment of Thy will.'

First, the voice of resignation. There is in all of us a lower will, a will of the flesh, which shrinks from pain and suffering. This will is not sinful; nor does it betoken a sinful nature. Christians need sometimes to be warned of this. They imagine that great sensibility to suffering, to bereavement, for instance, or bodily pain, or to the prospect of parting from friends, is incompatible with any high spiritual attainment. But this is a great mistake, against which Holy Scripture seems to enter its protest, when it says, 'No chastening for the present seemeth to be joyous, but grievous.' If it seemed to be joyous, or if it seemed to be anything but grievous, it would cease to be chastisement, and would fail to do the work of chastisement. The Stoics' mode of meeting trial was to freeze the heart, by considerations of reason, into insensibility, just as you may make the body callous by the application of ice. The Christian way of meeting it has always been, in imitation of the Master, to allow full play to the sensibilities, never to cramp the mind into the unnatural acknowledgment that pain is not painful, and at the same time to recognize in our heavenly Father a wiser and more loving will than our own, which 'makes all things work together for good to them that love Him.'

The Master in the garden showed Himself to be full of the acutest sensibility; His whole soul throbbed with pain, and recoiled with horror at the presentation to Him of the cup. 'Father, if it be possible,' He cried, as the great blood-drops of the agony chased one another down His gentle and majestic countenance, 'let this cup pass from Me.' But in the might of prayer, the higher will, the will of Christ's spirit, wrestled with and gained the mastery over the will of the flesh, which recoiled from suffering; and the second strong cry is thus worded (the difference is most instructive): 'O My Father, if this cup may not pass away from Me' (consistently, that is,

Thy Will be Done

with the great end of Thy glory and man's redemption) 'except I drink it, Thy will be done.' Here the Lord struck the keynote of Christian resignation for all His disciples to the end of time. 'I shrink from and deprecate trial. Nevertheless, if there be in the wise and loving counsels of My Heavenly Father a necessity for it, a design of grace towards Me or Mine, which cannot under the present economy and constitution of things be effectuated without it, then let it come to pass; I am willing that God should do what He wills with Me and upon Me.' Comfort, and cheerful, joyful acquiescence are found in the thought that God's will is the will of One whose name is light and love combined. Thinking of God merely as love, one might find a difficulty in some very stern and afflictive dispensation, which seems to yield no good result, but rather to sour the subjects of it, and to give others occasion to say, 'What profit is it to serve God?' But in these cases we turn with assurance to the sister statement that 'God is light.' We do not (and cannot) know all the circumstances of the case. We have no foresight into the future, no insight into the heart, no general survey of the marvellous and subtle links by which events are concatenated. If we had this, no doubt the God of love would be justified even to our eyes in His doing, and clear when He is judged. A father who, belated in the snow on a wintry night, should, without listening to their screams of fright, bury the bodies of his children in the snow, might not seem at first sight to be acting affectionately, and the children might struggle and cry, and imagine their father was murdering them. But this is only because the children are not aware that the snow acts as a warm mantle, and really cherishes the vital warmth in plants and animals which burrow in it. Had they this knowledge, the kindness of the father's action would be vindicated.

Secondly, the voice of dependence. 'This is the will of God,' says St. Paul, '*even your sanctification.*' Now in sanctification there is a twofold element, passive and active, which

Thy Will be Done 151

must be carefully kept in view, if we would embrace the whole truth. In one respect we are recipients in sanctification; in another we are agents. In order to the doing of a good action, or even to the thinking of a good thought, the preventing influence of the Holy Ghost must visit us, and the assisting influence of the same Spirit must work with us to produce the effect. Observe that we are so dependent upon God at every stage, that preventing, without assisting, grace is not sufficient. If only preventing grace is granted, there will be failure in the issue, just as when a potter's design is frustrated by his work being marred upon the wheel, and he throws aside as rubbish the mis-shapen vessel. By the grace of his Master preventing him, St. Peter walked for a few steps upon the water, but because that preventive grace did not assist him further, because he allowed unbelief to fill him with terror, so that he lost the assisting grace, he failed in the issue. When we pray, then, that God's will may be done in us, we ask to be made partakers of the preventing and assisting influences of the Holy Spirit, whereby alone our sanctification, which is God's will in us, can be wrought. And here again we recognize that the will of God is in accordance with His name or revealed character of light and love. For what is it to be sanctified, but to have the conscience filled with light, and the heart with love, by the grace of the Holy Spirit? A growing perception of the will of God as regards what He would have us to do, a growing appreciation of His perfections, and a growing sympathy with man for God's sake, these are sure signs of a progressive sanctification, which is nothing else than an increase of light and an increase of love.

But, thirdly, this petition is, in another aspect of it, the voice of holy energy. May 'Thy will be done,' not only concerning us in providence, not only within us in grace, but by us also in the active, hearty co-operation of our wills. These wills are created perfectly free; and their free unrestrained activity in the way of God's commandments—the surrender of them to Him as His instruments—is the last thing we ask in this petition. We, no less than the Spirit of God, must be agents in our own sanctification. That result is not any how to be attained without the concurrence of our own wills. Speculatively and in theory this is a great and perhaps insoluble mystery; practically it presents no difficulty at all. Something as nearly approaching to it as possible is seen in the natural life of man. Look at the operations of agriculture. Not all the toil in the world can make a blade of oats grow in the absence of the sun's warmth. If God withholds warmth, men and oxen may labour all the livelong day, and never raise a harvest. And yet if man neglected to scatter the seed and put his hand to the plough, or should even perform these operations carelessly and out of due season, the harvest would be equally frustrated. The concurrence of man's efforts with God's good blessing is essential in Nature to the production of the effect; and why not also in grace, of which Nature is in all her districts a parable? Then that our wills may yield to God's grace is one of the things solicited in the petition before us. And alas! who is there among us who, in this aspect of the petition, offers it with entire sincerity? How many good movements and instigations are constantly being made in our hearts by God's Spirit, and to how few of them do we respond with the whole energy of our wills! How little careful are we to turn to practical account on weekdays the good impressions we receive in God's house on Sundays! How thoroughly contented are we that a good impression should terminate upon itself! How do we welcome it with complacency as a favourable omen of our spiritual state, but never make an effort to bring it to good effect in our conduct! And this partly from pure indolence and that natural paralysis of the will which makes any exertion irksome; partly because, from the corruption of our nature, the active performance of God's will involves so very frequently the abnegation and thwarting of our own! 'If any man will come after Me,' says Christ, (literally 'willeth to come after Me'; and observe what the phrase imports),—'if any man willeth to come after Me,' let him not imagine that this will of the spirit will meet with no opposition or reluctance from the will of the flesh; on the contrary, let him prepare to encounter this opposition and to stand fast under it, 'let him deny himself, and take up his cross daily, and follow Me' (St. Luke ix. 23).

God's will be done! What a mockery that this petition should rest so constantly upon our lips, if whenever God's will thwarts ours, we choose ours in preference to His, and thus day after day speeds along without an attempt at self-denial, and while we profess (odious hypocrisy!) to be looking to His Cross for forgiveness, we never dream of taking up our own and bearing it after Him. And yet what inward peace would there be in bearing it! in annihilating our own will, so far as it is at all at variance with God's, and in seeking, with great simplicity and an entire unreservedness, to be and to do all that He would have us to be and to do! For the corrupt will of man is the source of all the discomposure and fretfulness which find place in the human heart. It is the deeply-seated source of sin, and therefore of labour and trouble.

Alas! how many are there who are more or less willing to acquiesce in God's dispensations, and more than willing, really desirous, to receive the gracious influences of God's Spirit, who have no mind at all to bestir themselves in the putting away of sin, in the correction of faults of character, in the amendment of bad habits, in the cultivation of Christian graces, in the attainment of holiness! To them the answer of God when they say, 'Thy will be done,' is that which He made to Joshua of old: 'Get thee up: wherefore liest thou thus upon thy face? ... There is an accursed thing in the midst of thee, O Israel: thou canst not stand before thine enemies, until ye take away the accursed thing from among you.' Therefore, Lord, give us grace to take away this accursed thing, our own corrupt will, which lusteth always contrary to Thy will. May each day witness some sacrifice of our will to Thine, so that henceforth we may say 'Thy will be done' with entire sincerity! For there is no day which brings not with it some opportunity for such a sacrifice.

> 'The trivial round, the common task,
> Will furnish all we need to ask;
> Room to deny ourselves, a road
> To bring us daily nearer God.'

CHAPTER IX

AS IN HEAVEN, SO IN EARTH

ANCIENT Fathers regarded this clause as qualifying the first three petitions of the Lord's Prayer, and not only the immediately foregoing one; so that we pray God for the hallowing of His name upon earth as it is hallowed in heaven, and for the coming of His kingdom upon earth as fully and universally as it is at present established in heaven, no less than for the doing of His will here as it is done in heaven above. And it would seem that the compilers of the English Catechism coincided with this view of the applicability of the clause. Their paraphrase of the first part of the Lord's Prayer is as follows: 'I desire my Lord God, our heavenly Father, who is the giver of all goodness, to send His grace unto me, and to all people; that we may worship Him, serve Him, and obey Him 'as we ought to do.' Here, '*that we may worship Him*' corresponds to ' Hallowed be Thy name'; and '*serve Him*' to 'Thy kingdom come'; and '*obey Him*' to 'Thy will be done'; while the phrase '*as we ought to do*' was no doubt intended to represent 'As in heaven, so in earth.' And '*as we ought to do*' must surely be intended to apply to the worship and service of God, as well as to the obedience which we owe Him. We pray for grace 'to worship Him (in our prayers),' and 'to serve Him (in our calling) as we ought to do,' no less than to 'obey Him (in our temptations) as we ought to do.

The opening invocation of the great Prayer draws up our eyes to heaven, the throne of God, and to Him who sitteth thereon; 'Our Father which art in Heaven.' There, first, our minds are occupied with God Himself, with His awful name, His majesty and His love; 'Hallowed be Thy name.' Next, the brilliant court, the glorious hierarchy of blessed and adoring angels, which surrounds the great Monarch, catches our mind's eye. We long that the same spectacle may meet our eyes, as in its chief seat, so in all the dependencies of the Almighty's vast empire. But here, alas! we discern many rebellious wills counteracting God's will, and actively thwarting His designs. Antagonism to heaven's Sovereign, with all its sad results of misery and disunion, is before our eyes as we look round; and we sigh for the harmony, order, obedience, of the heaven we have just left in thought. And so we pray, 'Thy will be done, as in heaven, so in earth.' Good quaint Bishop Andrewes, after the manner of the divines of that day, when it was not thought unseemly to provoke a smile from the pulpit, remarks, in making this clause the subject of a sermon, that 'adverbs please God better than verbs.' He means that God looks more to the manner in which we perform our actions than to the thing done; of which he says that this clause furnishes proof; for God bids us pray not simply that 'His will *may be done*,' but that it 'may be done *as it is in heaven*,' with fervour, alacrity, and love. And he goes on to observe that there are two qualifying clauses beginning with *As* in this Prayer, both of the greatest moment; for that, when God would teach us the homage and love we owe to Himself, He says it must be 'as in heaven,' after the model of angelic love and devotion; and when He would teach us what love we owe to our neighbour, He says it must be a love which forgives him, 'as' we desire to be forgiven ourselves. 'Forgive us our trespasses, as we forgive them that trespass against us.'

An excellent lesson; and it is well if the quaintness with which this holy and learned man has expressed it makes it cleave to the mind. The manner and measure of our obedience to God, the manner and measure of our love to our neighbour, are matters of prime importance. A stinted, grudging obedience, and a love which says that it forgives, while it makes no effort to forget, are no obedience and no love in God's eyes.

Let us consider then the words 'As in heaven' a little more closely. We use the term heaven in two senses. Sometimes we mean by it the material heaven, or firmament; sometimes the great temple of the universe, where God holds His court, and unveils His beauty to the hierarchy of the angels. Which of these is meant here? Probably both; but more particularly the latter. In the firmament or material heaven, God's will, whether ordinary or extraordinary, is uniformly and instantaneously done. All the aërial phenomena, lightning and hail, snow and vapours, wind and storm, fulfil the Lord's word. The planets revolve in their orbits, and obeying punctually the laws impressed upon them at their creation, ever display a spectacle of serene harmony and order. And even the exceptional cases when the master-hand of the creator and legislator interferes to suspend His own law, when these firmamental laws have been interrupted in their operations by the Divine will, as when sun and moon stood still at Joshua's bidding, as when the shadow went ten degrees backward at Hezekiah's prayer—these in the truest sense prove the rule. But the obedience of the heavenly bodies and the elements is, after all, not the obedience of free and accountable beings. Planets and elements must obey; they have no choice of their own; they are merely subject to mechanical or chemical laws. For the free, zealous, and loving obedience of rational creatures we must look above the firmamental heavens to the temple of the universe. It is to this temple, far above the material firmament, that our thoughts mount up in the petition before us. Yet it is worthy of remark that the lower or firmamental heaven is a striking type of the upper sanctuary, and shadows it forth to us, so far as things spiritual can be shadowed forth by things material. The powerful attraction by which the planets are tied to the sun, the serene harmony with which they all revolve around the sun, how beautiful an emblem is this of the gratitude and adoring love which keeps the unfallen angels in obedience to God, and of the order and harmony with which they encircle His throne; while their agency in executing His errands is compared to the subtlety, intensity, and potency of certain firmamental forces; 'He maketh His angels spirits (winds), and His ministers a flame of fire' (flashes of lightning); Ps. civ. 4.

It will be remembered that in the petition 'Thy will be done' we found a double meaning (pp. 49, 50). *'Be done'* might mean simply *'be carried into effect'*; in which case the petition would be the voice of acquiescence, or *'Be actively executed'*; in which case the petition would be the voice of holy energy. Both these meanings of the petition are to be carried into the qualification, 'As in heaven, so in earth.'

First, as to the active execution of God's will. We are taught in the Holy Scriptures to think of the service which holy angels do unto God, as consisting of two great elements, one of adoration and the other the execution of Divine messages (whence their name of angels or messengers). It is said of the seraphim, whom Isaiah saw in a vision, 'Each one had six wings; with twain he covered his face, and with twain he covered his feet' (in adoration of God and confession of the emptiness of a creaturely nature); 'and with twain he did fly'—speed to those parts of the world to which God commissioned

Him (Isa. vi. 2). Again; we read that in singing their 'Holy, holy, holy, Lord God Almighty,' they rest not day and night;—that their worship is unintermittent. Again; we are told of angels, who 'do always behold the face of My Father which is in heaven'; and Gabriel says of himself to Zacharias the priest, 'I am Gabriel, who stand in the presence of God,' intimating that the awe of the uncreated presence is always uppermost in angelic minds. Nor are they without the deepest interest in and sympathy with those rational creatures of God who are below them in the scale of creation, and below them also morally, as having fallen by sin, which holy angels never did. 'There is joy in heaven,' we are assured, 'over one sinner that repenteth'; they are all 'ministering spirits, sent forth to minister for them who shall be heirs of salvation,' and, emblematized by the golden cherubim who bent forward over the mercy-seat of the ark, 'they desire to look,' so Peter tells us, into the counsel of human redemption, as it is announced in the Gospel. Man's imitation of them, therefore, must consist in mingling the exercises of devotion with a punctual and zealous discharge of the duties of his position; in making haste, and delaying not the time, to keep God's commandments; in not merely doing, but in delighting to do, God's will; in constantly lifting up his heart to God day and night; in constantly striving to realize God's presence; and in sympathizing deeply with his fellow-men, and doing all in his power to succour them.

But when we pass from the thought of active obedience to that of submission, which indeed is (rather than the other) the force of the original words, how shall we here find any model among the angels? How can angels practise submission to God's will? Strangers to sin, and therefore strangers to sorrow, how can they set us an example of acquiescence in all which Divine Providence prescribes? And another thought intrudes to make us seek some other specimen of conformity to Divine will, besides that which the angels furnish. The angels have a nature more exalted and more spiritual than our own. They have never known the trials and infirmities involved in a body of humiliation, and in a pilgrimage through human life. Their condition has, as far as it is revealed to us, never been debased and debilitated by a fall. Altogether, they belong to another and higher order of beings. And thus their example in the abstract seems absolutely beyond our reach. What we want to see for our encouragement is an angelic life led upon earth by a Son of Man. Well, God points us to just such a life in the career of Jesus of Nazareth. The zeal, the love, the fervour, the spirituality, the sympathy, the activity of a heavenly Being He brought down to earth, and illustrated with the utmost beauty under the conditions of humanity. Speaking of Him by prophetic anticipation, the Psalmist said, 'I have set *God always before me.*' His inner communion with His heavenly Father, even when overcast for a time by a cloud of dreadful darkness, as it was upon the cross, was always profound and unintermittent. Intense was the zest and zeal, with which He addressed Himself to His great mission: 'My meat,' said He, 'is to do the will of Him that sent Me.' And His deep and universal sympathy with men was such, that He frequented all companies, had an ear for every tale of woe, and a heart filled to overflowing with sensibility to sorrows ; while the succour, which invariably accompanied His sympathy was so liberally extended, that His entire course is described by this feature of it : ' He went about doing good.'

Nor were His vast philanthropic labours accounted by Him any exemption from the duties of devotion. With Him long days of teaching, and working cures, were succeeded by nights of prayer. A higher than angelic devotion alternated with or pervaded a higher than angelic industry. But His passive graces were, if possible, even more conspicuous than His active. As being the seed of the woman, not of the man, He was the first hero who ever gave prominence to the feminine virtues of meek, unresisting endurance. A death of cruelty, vilification, and outrage He met without a murmur on His own account, with ejaculations of affiance in God, with considerateness for those whom He was leaving behind, with a prayer for His murderers, and with an infinitely consolatory assurance to a poor penitent who was hanging at His side and struggling back, as best He might, to God. And in the garden of Gethsemane, when His pure soul recoiled with shuddering from the cup of woe which He was about to drink, He still took up in His own behalf, and led the way in offering, the prayer which He had placed in the mouth of His disciples. 'Father,' said He, with all the sensibility of flesh and blood, and yet in all the meekness of a perfect submission, 'if this cup may not pass away from Me except I drink it, Thy will be done' (St. Matt. xxvi. 42). So illustrious an example of conformity to God's will throws even angelic obedience into the shade, while at the same time it introduces into this conformity the idea of resignation which is exclusively His own, as well as that of obedience, in which angels too, though in a lower degree, are our models.

A grand and elevating thought arises now, viz. that God would have us walk in the steps of our father Abraham, to whom it was said, 'Walk before Me, and be thou perfect'; that we should aspire to nothing short of perfection. If He teaches us to pray that His name may be hallowed, His kingdom come, His will be done, 'in earth, as it is in heaven'— if He teaches us to request that the zeal and love, which animated the human heart of the Redeemer, may be reproduced in us by His Spirit —He unmistakably enforces this truth, that Christians are required to aim deliberately at the highest of all standards. The acquiescence then in a regular and devout exterior, which thousands are so ready to yield; the dead level of piety and good conduct on which many are content to pace up and down, like a sentinel on a platform, rather than a soldier scaling a citadel, is emphatically protested against in the Lord's Prayer.

The better sort of people may perhaps be divided into two classes, those who set before themselves a high standard but fail to reach it, and those whose standard is very low and who do in the main come up to it. The latter class plume themselves occasionally on their common sense, their moderation, their avoidance of all extravagances, their knowledge of human life and character. 'You may preach for ever,' they say, 'but you will never make men angels; you cannot get an Act of Parliament' (the most potent force such persons can conceive of) 'to alter human nature. Let your exhortations to virtue and godliness be vague and general; let them not pierce too much to the quick, or go into men's manner of life too minutely and microscopically; let them not be chivalrous and Quixotic (for if they are, people will give them up as hopeless), but modest and practicable; let them inculcate strict honesty in money matters, honourable conduct in society, moral regularity (at least when the heyday of youthful passions is over), regularity in attending church on Sundays (except when one happens to be abroad), all this mixed up with a good flavour of religious sentiment—do what you will, you will never get much beyond this—rest in it, and be thankful.'

But verily, in spite of such faithless discouragements, every time they take this Prayer into their lips, they make a solemn profession before God that the devotion, the zeal, the obedience, the submission at which they are aiming, is that which is exemplified in heaven, by the holy angels and by our Lord Himself. For what a shocking inconsistency (that I may not say, what an awful mockery) must it be for a man deliberately to ask God in the morning that His will 'may be done on earth, as it is in heaven,' and then as deliberately to pass all the rest of the day without a single effort to become more obedient to His will than he has been for months past And yet how many are there who never make any such effort; who are perhaps quite willing to place their standard as high as the society in which they move has placed it conventionally, quite willing to be church-goers, promoters of good objects, thinkers and talkers about religion, but, alas! not willing to try to lead an angelic life upon earth, or (in other and better words) to be conformed to the mind of Christ.

There are two elements in this unwillingness. One is a mere indisposition to rouse themselves for any high achievement; and it is to be met by considering that our Lord represents '*striving*' (or agonizing) to enter in at the strait gate, as distinct from '*seeking*,' to be a condition of success, and that St. Paul even implies the possibility of running (or making considerable exertions) in the heavenly race, while yet the runner shall not so run as to obtain. The other is a secret distrust of God, as if His mercy could not blot out any sins, and His grace could not achieve any victory in us; a vain and foolish notion that they who do obtain the prize in the heavenly race start with some natural qualifications in themselves, with a little stock-in-trade of strength and virtue, which less favoured persons do not possess. They have to learn that St. Paul is announcing a real and vital truth, not putting aside out of false modesty an honour he was justly entitled to, when he says, after glancing at his more abundant labours, 'Yet not I, but the grace of God which was with me.'

But anyhow they are condemned out of their own mouth when they say, 'As in heaven, so in earth.' None live up to this clause who cannot both sigh and aspire with the Apostle—sigh with him after this manner, 'O wretched man that I am! who shall deliver me from the body of this death'—or aspire as he did,

'Not as though I had already attained, either were already perfect: but I follow after, if that I may apprehend that for which also I am apprehended of Christ Jesus. Brethren, I count not myself to have apprehended: but this one thing I do, forgetting those things which are behind, and reaching forth unto those things which are before, I press toward the mark for the prize of the high calling of God in Christ Jesus' (Phil. iii. 12-14).

CHAPTER X

GIVE US THIS DAY OUR DAILY BREAD

WE now come to the second part of the Lord's Prayer. Leaving the worship pure and simple of the first part, passing through the transition clause, 'Thy will be done in earth, as in heaven,' we arrive at petition pure and simple (see ch. i). We are to *worship* before we *pray*. It is after the adoration of God's character, after aspirations for His kingdom and will, that the voice of human necessity—the humble statement of man's many and pressing needs—sounds forth in this second section of the Prayer.

Man's life upon earth is lived in time, or, in other words, his existence is meted out to him in successive portions; life is one continual passage out of the past into the future over the bridge of the present. The divisions of this latter part of the Prayer, then, correspond to these divisions of human life. First, we recognize the need of the present, 'Give us *this day* our daily bread.' But our life had a yesterday, and its yesterday was stained by sins, and is the subject of regretful retrospect. That yesterday's evil may be cancelled by the pure grace and mercy of Him who promises, 'I, even I, am He that blotteth out thy transgressions for mine own sake, and will not remember thy sins' (Isa. xliii. 25); wherefore this is our second suit unto God, '*Forgive us our trespasses.*' But as there was a yesterday in our life, so, if God should grant us the support which we first sued for, there will be a to-morrow. In the view of this to-morrow, therefore, we pray that God would not allow it to bring an unduly heavy trial, and would preserve us from that sin in future, which we trust that He has forgiven in the past. '*Lead us not into temptation; but deliver us,*' &c.

It may possibly be asked, 'Why is not forgiveness asked for in the first instance before bread?' The Daily Morning and Evening Office of the Book of Common Prayer begin most appropriately with a confession of sins and an absolution; and it would certainly seem as if nothing were more necessary for a sinner, in his approach to the Throne of Grace, than the pardon of his offences. Yet the placing pardon first among our needs would interfere with the order of thought in this latter part of the Prayer, and would be untrue to the phenomena of our mental constitution. By the constitution of the human mind, the present is to every man the most instant, urgent part of human life; it is ever vividly before one, while the memory of the past is fast fading away, and the hope of the future is not yet realized. The needs, therefore, of the present day, as affecting not only the body but the mind most vividly, figure first in our order of petition. And there would appear to be another reason for this priority. The Apostle says, ' Howbeit that was not first which is spiritual, but that which is natural; and afterward,' &c. (1 Cor. xv. 46). Adam was before Christ, and the natural man is the basis upon which the spiritual man is by grace grafted. Bread (in the primary and simple meaning of the word) is a want of the body—a desire of the natural man. Forgiveness and grace are wants of the soul—desires of the spiritual man. Therefore as that which was natural was first in the order of God's creation, the petition for the *natural* blessing comes in God's Prayer before the petition for the *spiritual*[1].

[1] We cannot surely (with a certain class of interpreters, at the head of whom must needs stand St. Jerome) consent to exclude from this petition any reference to man's natural wants, however much we may include under it a reference to our spiritual wants. Because by bread the Lord intended us to understand the bread of the Word and that of the Sacraments, we may not therefore conclude that He intended to shut out the word 'bread' from its literal commonplace meaning. Such a conclusion is forbidden, if by nothing else, yet certainly by a great canon of interpretation which applies to the entire volume of Holy Scripture, and especially to its deeper parts, viz. that the limitation of any text to one particular meaning is contrary to the mind of the Holy Ghost, whose method is to put into all His utterances a fullness and multiplicity of meaning, all in dependence upon the primary meaning, and without excluding it. So that the Holy Scriptures resemble those living creatures in the Book of Revelation (iv. 6) who were 'full of eyes before and behind' (the eye being that which gives expression and meaning to the countenance). Therefore we should always prefer the richer and fuller view of any

Observe, then, that the Prayer has now sunk to the lowest point which it is ever to reach. We have been in heaven hitherto, contemplating God's character, surveying the seat of His vast empire and the allegiance of the blessed angels to His will. Now we have descended to the earth, and to the level of man's lowest wants.

passage of Scripture to that which is narrower, remembering that though in the intention of the human writer the application of his words may have been merely contextual and limited to the local temporary circumstances of which he was writing, yet in the purview of the Holy Spirit, under whose impulse he wrote, many other applications of the words may have been designed, many other circumstances foreseen to which they were meant to refer. And to the Lord's Prayer, in which we have to do not only with a human writer but with a Divine Speaker, whose words the human writer records, this remark will especially apply. Nor does it seem that St. Jerome was led to his view of an exclusively spiritual application of this petition by any other reason than a misunderstanding of the word which in our version is rendered 'daily.' His rendering was 'supersubstantial,' which seems to him to mean that the bread spoken of was other than natural bread—a view to which the devout author of the *Christian Year* has given both weight and currency—

'Nor by our daily bread mean common food.'

Suffice it to say that the word could hardly have the meaning attributed to it.

For bread or food is a want which we share with the beasts which perish. And not only so. We share with them in a certain sense the expression of this want. 'The lions,' we read, 'roaring after their prey, do seek their meat from God' (Ps. civ. 21). And again, 'He giveth fodder unto the cattle, and feedeth the young ravens that call upon Him' (Ps. cxlvii. 9).

We must not reason away the force of these expressions. The lower creatures have certain needs, and God has given them certain organs for the utterance of those needs. Their voice, though of course not consciously or deliberately addressed to Him, yet excites the fatherly compassion of their Creator, who pities them, and places their food in their way. In the petition before us we have man, who is able to recognize the Giver, and to make conscious and deliberate application to Him, uttering his needs rationally, as the lower creatures do by inarticulate cries. How truly is this a prayer for man, representing his relations to, and expressing his sympathies with, all creation. After we have aspired to be as angels in the doing of God's will, we sink to the level of the lowest creatures, and sue for daily bread. And is it not the very truth of our condition, that we *are* akin to the angels by our immortal spirits, and to the beasts that perish by our animal nature? Is not man, as a fact, a very microcosm, touching heaven and earth at the same time? Endowed with a mind which can compute the motions of stars, and can flash its ideas upon an electric wire through tunnelled mountains and along the bed of oceans, and still higher, with a spirit which can hold communion with God and reflect His image—he is yet as dependent upon daily food as the meanest reptile which crawls upon the earth, and has as great necessity to cry to God for it.

And this daily sustenance we beseech our Father to give us.

1. God, then, is the Giver of bread, even though He may give it, as He does most other blessings, by secondary and instrumental causes. But alas! how often have we asked Him to give it, without any cordial acknowledgement of our dependence upon Him for it! In the mouth of a very poor man, whose wages scarcely serve to

supply a large family with a bare maintenance, and who, when thrown out of work by illness, feels how utterly dependent he is upon health and strength, this 'give' has no doubt something of reality. But the easy competence which most of us enjoy leads us to regard our food as a matter of course; money, we think, can command all things; and if there is a sure supply of money, food at all events is felt to be at our command. The asking God to give it, when we have much goods laid up for many years, is too apt to degenerate into a hollow form. And whenever this state of mind is extensively prevalent in a nation; when all classes of men above the very lowest begin to trust in uncertain riches rather than in the living God, who giveth us all things richly to enjoy; then God breaks the staff of bread, in one of the thousand ways in which He may break it, by sending a succession of bad harvests, or withholding the rain or the sunshine, or by sending a murrain among the cattle, or an enemy to intercept our imports from abroad. Affluent persons then begin to learn what is overlooked in the maxim that money can command all things, namely, that it can only command such things as can be had by payment for them; that gold and silver are not articles of nourishment, and cannot be converted into articles of nourishment where there is a failure of those articles in the market. And by casualties of another kind, such as the breaking of banks and the failure of speculations, God teaches that, even if money could command all things, the possessors of money cannot always rely on money. How many have learned by painful experience the insecurity of worldly wealth—a truth as old as Solomon, but hitherto a dead letter to them; but then, a living reality. 'Labour not to be rich: cease from thine own wisdom. Wilt thou set thine eyes upon that which is not? for riches certainly make themselves wings; they fly away, as an eagle toward heaven' (Prov. xxiii. 4, 5).

2. 'Give us.' We have no warrant in this divine prayer for praying, 'Give ME this day *my* bread.' The bread which God gives me is *ours*, not *mine*. Other people have a right in it, a claim upon it, as well as I myself. It is more

a common than a private stock. I must therefore acknowledge my brother's claim and right, by dealing my bread to the hungry, and giving to him that needeth. If I do not this, or do it not to the extent of my ability, it is a mere mockery to ask God to 'give *us* bread.' In that case I *speak* of the bread as being something given for the benefit of all, and I *treat* it as something given for my own special and exclusive benefit. And this is the hypocrisy condemned by St. James of saying to a brother or sister, who is naked and destitute of daily food, 'Depart in peace, be ye warmed and filled,' while we 'give them not those things which are needful for the body.'

In the first fervours of Christian faith, the Church realized so vividly the truth that the bread which God gives is a common stock, designed for His whole family, that none of the Jerusalem Christians 'said that ought of the things which he possessed was his own; but they had all things common. Neither was there any among them that lacked: for as many as were possessors of lands or houses sold them, and brought the prices of the things that were sold, and laid them down at the Apostles' feet: and distribution was made unto every man according as he had need' (Acts iv. 32, 34, 35). This was a beautiful glimpse, evanescent as a dissolving view, of the sympathy between classes which would prevail in the Church of Christ if she reached the Master's great ideal of her.

Community of goods, as an obligatory enactment imposed from without, would obliterate that distinction of poor and rich which is part of the present divinely appointed economy of probation for all classes, while at the same time it would leave entirely untouched the selfishness at the bottom of the human heart. But community of goods, brought about by the spontaneous sympathy of Christians with their fellow-Christians, the uncoerced expression of a family feeling towards all who are of the household of faith and for whom Christ died— this is the lofty standard of practice to which we should endeavour to approximate, and to adjust our sentiments as well as approximate our conduct. For the mere large giving to objects of charity is, after all, not so very difficult an attainment. Men may give largely, as feeling themselves in duty bound to do so, and as discharging the responsibilities of wealth. And yet they may fail entirely to give in that sympathizing spirit which recognizes the poor as brethren and members of one family with us of whom Christ is the Head. Alms are too often given as an act of grace towards persons of a lower caste, rather than from the fellow-feeling of a community in the household of Christ, such as leads us to embrace others with ourselves in our prayers.

3. *'This day'*; or, as St. Luke has it somewhat more emphatically, *'day by day.'* Teaching us in a most significant way that prayer is to be offered daily; that our dependence upon God is from day to day. There is something here of great doctrinal and practical import. We might suppose that God gave us a lease of life once for all at our birth, set the animal economy in motion originally, and then left it to work on till, in His appointed time, it should run down. But the Scriptures give another

representation of the case. They say that we are momentarily dependent upon God for all the functions of animal life; that 'in Him we live, and move, and have our being'; that 'He giveth to all men life, and breath, and all things' (Acts xvii. 25, 28)—breath, i.e. not merely a certain span, but each successive act by which the span is prolonged. Our dependence upon God, then, being continual, our acknowledgement must be continual also—must be made 'day by day.' It would not be suitable, or meet the truth of the facts, to go to God once for all, and say, 'Heavenly Father, give me bread for the term of my natural life.' If God supports us day by day, He must be sued day by day to do it. Besides, in a world of uncertainties like this, we can only see just what lies under our hand. We live for the day only; and so, if God should grant us to-day provision for the morrow, it might be superfluous, because 'we know not what shall be on the morrow.' For 'what is your life? It is even a vapour, that appeareth for a little time and then vanisheth away.' 'This night' our 'soul' may 'be required.'

There is a most striking illustration in the ancient law of the 'day by day' in this petition. The manna is expressly called by Moses, 'the bread which the Lord hath given you to eat.' It fell from heaven, without any human agency, and so proclaimed itself to the senses to be (what all food is, even though given by secondary causes) the gracious gift of God Himself. The people were instructed to gather it *every morning*; to take neither more nor less than an omer for every man, in which case it exactly supplied the needs of their families; and *not to leave any portion of what they gathered until the morning*. May we not say that the whole doctrine of human sustenance is here comprehended? First, our sustenance is the gift of God, though it may come to us by human exertion, and through the intervention of natural causes. Secondly, it is to be sought of God, as the manna was, *every morning*; 'Give us *day by day* our daily bread.' Thirdly, we are to seek a sufficient supply, and not a superfluous one; we are not to ask that which may be laid up for the morrow, but only enough for the day.

Would that we could enter more fully into the spirit of this 'day by day'! How few in that case would our anxieties be compared with what they are! Every day is, in the view of Holy Scripture, rather a distinct pilgrimage in itself than a distinct stage in one great pilgrimage. Each day brings with it its own responsibilities, its own trials, its own cares. Sufficient unto each day, as our Lord warns us, is the evil thereof. As regards foresight of the future, and a due provision against its contingencies, of course it would be an abdication of the prerogative of reason, which could not possibly be pleasing to God, if we did not exercise such foresight and make such provision to the best of our ability. God reproves such want of foresight by referring us to the instinct of the irrational creatures: 'Go to the ant, thou sluggard; consider her ways, and be wise: which having no guide, overseer, or ruler, provideth her meat in the summer, and gathereth her food,' &c. (Prov. vi. 6-8). But even if He did not expressly reprove it, could we doubt what His mind was? What makes the difference between the savage and the civilized man, but that the first subsists uncertainly from day to day on the food which he hunts or snares; the other deliberates for an unseen future, and sees his way, under God's blessing, to harvests, or to the revenue of handicrafts? And must we not believe that the structure of civilization is reared under a divine instinct, and has the sanction of Him who implanted in man the faculty which looks before and after?

But rational provision against the future is one thing; anxious care for the future, as if God could not and would not provide for the tomorrow of His children, is quite another. And it is this anxious care—not a want of energy in improving our resources—which is the great snare of our country and our times. The temptation naturally incidental to all high civilization is a trust in human foresight, and in the protections and provisions which it is able to make for the security and well-being of society. But this trust, singularly unlike trust in God, does not give peace to the heart. On the contrary, it is connected with a profound feeling of insecurity, and with a fever of restlessness. For a little experience of life suffices to prove that, even under the most favourable circumstances, human securities are insecure.

To realize our day-by-day dependence upon God, if so be we have first made the sincere acknowledgement of His name as 'Our Father which is in heaven,' would be the antidote of this feverish, unsettling, false trust. To leave to-morrow, after we had made all reasonable provision, in His hands, who is too loving a Father to deny us anything that is for our good, too wise to allow us anything that is mischievous; to throw the future entirely upon His providential care; to make up our spiritual accounts at nightfall as exactly as if we were not to wake from our sleep, and as if therefore provision for to-morrow would be superfluous;— this is to live in the spirit of the petition, 'Give us this day our daily bread'; in the spirit of the precept, 'Be careful for nothing; but in every thing by prayer and supplication with thanksgiving let your requests be made known unto God' (Phil. iv. 6).

CHAPTER XI

OUR DAILY BREAD

THE three last words of the petition are assuredly no less rich in lessons of wisdom than those which engaged our attention in the last chapter. 'Our' is the first of these words. What does it imply? Man has not only the use of bread by God's gracious grant of it, he can also establish in it a certain right and property. How, then, does bread become our own? The plain answer is, By working for it. St. Paul says, with a special emphasis upon the 'own,' as strongly marked in the original as it is in the translation, 'Even when we were with you, this we commanded you, that if any would not work, neither should he eat. For we hear that there are some which walk among you disorderly, working not at all, but are busybodies. Now them that are such we command and exhort by our Lord Jesus Christ, that with quietness they work, and eat their own bread' (2 Thess. iii. 10–12). And the promise of God by the Psalmist is: 'Thou shalt eat' (not bread, which drops into thy mouth with no exertion of thine own, but) 'the labour of thine hands' (Ps. cxxviii. 2). And this annexation of bread to honest toil is of very early date; it traces back to the fall of man, when God said to Adam, as a sentence indeed, but a sentence largely qualified by mercy, 'In the sweat of thy face thou shalt eat bread.' What an important element in the petition this little 'our' is! For, in the absence of it, men might so look upon God as the Bread-Giver, as to hope that He would supply them without their own exertions; but no! every time you recite the Lord's Prayer you imply that you will do your part in procuring the bread—for you may not pray, 'Give us this day daily bread,' but 'Give us this day OUR daily bread,' even that which we have earned and established a sort of claim to.

But it may be asked how we propose to make this doctrine of the necessity of labour universally applicable. Are there not many, it will be said, who are born in such circumstances that they can eat bread to the full without labouring to earn it? And is it not a condition of any high state of civilization that there should be many who are exempt altogether from the necessity of working for their livelihood? No doubt this is so; and since the accumulation of property and wealth in the hands of those of superior ability to their fellows, and their descendants, is a necessary condition, under the present constitution of things, of the balance of society, and the balance of society must clearly be in accordance with the will of God, the exemption of some from the necessity of labour must be viewed as an arrangement of God's good providence. But allowing all this, it still remains true that no man on earth, be his station what it may, is exempt in point of conscience from the obligation of beneficial labour. Industry is an universal obligation. God will tolerate no drones in His hive; and the millionaire and the man of broad acres must work (as very many, indeed the majority, of such persons do) for the good of all, though not for their own maintenance. There are great provinces of good work appointed to be done, for they cannot otherwise be done at all, by men of independent means, who need not to be paid for their services. Indeed, all voluntary work is costly. It is one of the inestimable advantages of independent means as a gift of God, that it enables some of the very highest work to be done to the glory of God from the highest of all motives, the love of God.

But alas! looking at this sacred obligation, which lies upon all, to work in some form or shape for others, if not for themselves, how appalling is the thought of the precious hours squandered by many, rich and poor alike, in merest idleness or dissipation, and not unfrequently in a deliberate attempt to kill time! How many days are spent by people of refinement, high position, and easy circumstances, of which, if a candid retrospect were made at night, the record in the journal would be,

'I have done nothing in the smallest degree useful to-day, nothing which could by possibility improve either my own spirit or the condition of those around me.' How many days are spent by people who ought to labour for their livelihood, and do not, in lamentable indolence, and even attacks upon the industry of their industrious neighbours! It is no small mercy to be exempt from the easy liability of falling into sin so grievous, by the actual pressure of employment in order to maintenance. Let us not covet for ourselves, or for those in whom we are interested, a position dangerously independent of honest toil. Labour in the work of a regular calling for the man, the labour of keeping house and the home-life of the family for the woman, is an enormous blessing. It keeps the mind bright, elastic, and free from morbid fancies. It makes rest and recreation a real pleasure, both in prospect and enjoyment. It sweetens the bread that is earned by it, while at the same time it does not make us less liberal in distributing it; for experience often shows that the earners of money with the brain are more generous in giving it than those who are born to it. It opens a clear path in which to serve God without perplexity or scruple. It is in the primitive and natural course of things; and therefore happier in the long run, and more exempt from trial, than a condition of things which results from civilization, and so from artificial causes.

The next word is 'daily.' In the original it is a very peculiar word, not found in the New Testament except in the Lord's Prayer, never found in the Septuagint (i.e. in the Greek translation of the Old Testament used by our Lord and His Apostles), and never found in classical Greek. The word is unique, used only on this occasion. The interpretation most generally received by modern scholars is that which regards the word as expressing the opposite of one etymologically connected with it, which means 'superfluous.' Thus it would mean enough for our needs, and not more than enough. Our necessities are variable and depend on a thousand circumstances, over which we have little or no control. The habits in which we have been bred and reared, the amount of education we have received, the temperament which we have derived from Nature, the position which we hold in society, the sensitiveness of our minds and bodies, all affect our necessities. We ask God in these words to furnish us with resources, not according to some fixed standard, but according to those peculiar needs of our own which He best knows, who reads our hearts and surveys our circumstances. And of all our *genuine* needs we may confidently expect a supply from His fatherly goodness. But anything beyond these needs we have no warrant for asking, or even seeking. The fever fit of competition incidental to a high state of civilization, the labouring to be rich, nay very rich, so as entirely to distance our neighbours in the furniture of our establishments, the sumptuousness of our equipages, the ostentatiousness of our hospitality, the multiplication of property beyond the demands of reason and modesty, the seeking to 'join house to house, to lay field to field, till there be no place, that we may be placed alone in the midst of the earth' (Isa. v. 8),—all this is condemned at once and for ever by the utter simplicity and modesty of the petition, 'Give us this day our *sufficient* (or *adequate*) supply of bread.' What a mockery is it so to pray morning by morning, while in the actual commerce of life our whole mind is bent on obtaining—not competency for us and ours, but opulence; not a modest position, suitable to our abilities, where we may serve God quietly in our generation, but high place, large means, and positions of influence. It ought to shame us to reflect that, long ages before the Lord's Prayer, with all the sacred and beautiful lessons involved in it, was given to the world, a holy man of God, who lived in the dim light of the elder dispensation, would ask no more of worldly goods at God's hands than this: 'Give me neither poverty nor riches; feed me with food convenient for me: lest I be full, and deny Thee, and say, Who is the Lord? or lest I be poor, and steal, and take the name of my God in vain' (Prov. xxx. 8).

'Bread' is the last word in this petition. And it carries on the lesson of the foregoing word, the lesson that we should restrain our desires for earthly things to that which is seen by our Heavenly Father to be needful for the comfortable maintenance and preservation of life. But of which life? For into man at his creation there was breathed—not the breath of life, but 'the breath of lives.' Man lives a spiritual or supernatural, as well as an animal or natural, life. And therefore however much we may protest against the limitation, which has been made by St. Jerome and others, of this word 'bread' to our spiritual sustenance, we would insist with equal earnestness that this higher food must be comprehended under the term 'bread.' Surely our bread, as Bishop Andrewes remarks, is not exclusively that animal nourishment which is common to us and the inferior creatures. Man's food must be something nobler than the food of cattle; it must be 'panis angelorum'—angels' food. This 'angels' food' is the Bread of God, 'which cometh down from heaven, and giveth life unto the world'

(St. John vi. 33)—the personal Word of God, who bears up the pillars of the universe, 'upholding all things by the word of His power' (Heb. i. 3), and who for our sake became incarnate and was made 'a little lower than the angels' (Heb. ii. 9), in order that He might fulfil God's law, and endure its penalty of death, and then give Himself to sinners as a suitable nourishment for their souls. And now, by His incarnation and propitiatory death, having become the Bread of Life, He offers Himself to us for the sustenance of our spiritual life, to be received under the outward elements of food and drink.

The Holy Eucharist is the means ordained by Himself to be the means of partaking of His Body and Blood, which 'except ye eat and drink,' said He, 'ye have no life in you.'

This Bread of heaven is the primary bread we seek, and therefore in this petition of the Lord's Prayer we should particularly think (as it appears the framers of the primitive liturgies did think) of the Eucharistic Bread when we use this petition. We should remind ourselves what grievous symptoms of declension from primitive fervour most Churchmen exhibit in contenting themselves with at most a weekly (instead of, as it was in primitive times, a daily) celebration of this most comfortable Sacrament; and we should mentally make this petition a sort of preparatory prayer for our next communion, without losing sight of the protest underlying the word 'daily.'

This petition, moreover, must be held to place the same restriction upon our desires for spiritual, as on those for animal, sustenance. Every thing which contributes to the maintenance, vigour, and well-being of spiritual life we may confidently ask of God; but as for spiritual dainties, spiritual luxuries, spiritual stimulants, spiritual sensations, spiritual excitements—in what light do these appear when compared with the grave, quiet modesty of the petition, 'Give us this day our daily bread'?

And yet the religious public, of all schools and parties, ever lusts after a dressing and serving up of true religion with condiments, which may stimulate the dull palate, and give a relish to the old and (as they are accounted) somewhat stale truths of the Bible and Prayer Book. What a great distastefulness prevails for the solid and the sound in sermons and religious works! What applause is immediately won by a writer or a preacher who commits himself to clever, brilliant, flippant views of God's provision of spiritual support, His holy Word and Sacraments! Then, because the ordinary routine of worship and instruction, as carried on in our churches, is not exciting or stirring enough, we must forsooth convene our congregations in showrooms and theatres, where the familiar liturgy may be dispensed with, and where devotional exercises may gain a zest from the strangeness and unsuitableness of their surroundings. And probably in the movement known as Ritualistic, though here doubtless there are other and deeper principles at work, there is a popular element of the same description, a weariness of approved religious methods as flat and dull, and an attempt to season more highly the dish for the spiritual palate, by striking novelties, or by appeals to the imagination and the senses. The petition for 'daily bread' condemns the lust after such novelties. We do not want, for the maintenance and growth of our spiritual life, and we have no warrant for seeking, fascinations, or ecstasies, or devotional raptures, or fits of spiritual enthusiasm. We need not to be galvanized into spiritual emotions; all that we want is spiritually to 'live by the faith of the Son of God, who loved us, and gave Himself for us' (Gal. ii. 20). We want indeed to grow in the knowledge of God, by practising our present knowledge, steadily, quietly, consistently, and with much fewer vacillations of the will than at present. All that can really contribute to this end of our hopes and efforts, we find in the Bible and Prayer Book. If effervescence of feeling can be shown really to conduce to growth in faith and love, we would willingly embrace all or any of its means. But if none of them can claim to do more than supply a stimulant for spiritual sensations, then we say that what we are in search of is nourishment, not stimulants, and we fall back on our Lord's Prayer and the exposition of it in our Catechism. 'I pray unto God that He will send us all things that be needful both for our souls and bodies.'

> 'Faith's meanest deed more favour bears
> Where hearts and wills are weighed,
> Than brightest transports, choicest prayers,
> Which bloom their hour, and fade.'

CHAPTER XII

AND FORGIVE US OUR DEBTS

We come now to the first of those conjunctions by which the latter section of the Prayer, unlike the former, is knit together. 'Give us this day our daily bread; and' (lest daily bread should prove a curse rather than a blessing) 'give us' therewithal 'daily pardon of our transgressions.' Nothing is more demonstrable than that the supply of our daily wants, if unaccompanied with an outflow of God's pardoning mercy, would be a curse, and a heavy one. For imagine everything necessary to the maintenance of this life to be given without this outflow! In that case our trespass accumulates every day, and there is no act of grace running parallel with it to expunge it.

And possibly there is another implication in

the 'and,' as though it was said, 'Give us this day our daily bread, and' (that we may be able to enjoy the blessings we have asked for, let us taste also of Thy mercy) 'forgive us our debts.' A full and high relish for God's natural blessings there is not, and cannot be, without an experience and an appreciation of His pardoning mercy. The want of it would taint all the rest. While, on the other hand, this experience and appreciation gives a zest even to those common and trivial pleasures of life which the natural man takes as a matter of course, and thinks it a hardship to be deprived of. A fair landscape borrows double beauties when it is seen in the light of God's pardoning love in Christ. It is the mind and heart of the spectator which impart to the landscape its charms. To one of the lower animals, who wants intelligence, a lake and an alp tinted with the sunset is nothing more than any other sight; it awakes no emotion, it excites no admiration. To a man of refined mind and cultivated feeling, on the other hand, the sight of the lake or the alp is a high and pure enjoyment. Now the Christian's mind has received refinement, and the Christian's heart cultivation, from the light and love of God which have been poured into them. In looking at the alp and the lake and the sunset, we can say, 'My Father made them all'; and the same Father forgives me my debts. The thought lends them a beauty which otherwise they would lack, for the mind tinges Nature with its own hues. And, on the other hand, who has not heard the tale, so strikingly illustrative of the connexion of thought we are tracing, of a discontented and fretful man, who, sauntering about in his peevishness, strayed by a poor hovel, and on looking through the casement saw a miserable creature in tatters with a loaf of coarse brown bread in his hand? He was about to eat it; but before doing so the observer saw that he raised his eyes, which were filled with tears, to heaven, and ejaculated, 'All this Thou givest me, and Christ besides.' 'Is he so thankful only for a coarse loaf?' thought the observer. Yes! the mercy of God, which this poor soul had tasted, had sweetened to him the coarsest fare. He well understood that the most delicate bread could not be truly enjoyed without mercy, and that with mercy even the coarsest bread becomes a dainty. In short, he knew what the AND meant in 'Give us this day our daily bread, AND forgive us our trespasses.'

But now to the petition itself. 'Forgive us our trespasses'; literally, 'Remit to us, discharge us from, our debts.' In the version of the Lord's Prayer, as given by St. Luke, the word is 'sins'—'Forgive us our sins.' But even here, in the qualifying clause, the image of a debt appears; 'for we also forgive every one that is indebted to us' (lit. 'for we also discharge every one that owes us aught'). We have also the parable of the two debtors, in which man's offences against God and against his fellow-man are represented respectively as heavy and slight debts. We may say therefore that our blessed Lord studiously represents sin as a debt, and would have us think of it under that figure. The figure, therefore, must be instructive; and we must endeavour to draw forth the lessons suggested by it.

First remark that this is a figure of common parlance—a figure which has wrought itself into the texture of the language of daily life. For what do we mean when we say, 'I *ought* to do such and such a thing'; 'I did wrong, and I *ought* to be punished for it.' 'Ought' is originally and fundamentally the perfect tense of the verb 'to owe'; and, therefore, when we say, 'I ought to do this,' 'I ought to be punished for not doing it,' what we mean is that such an action or piece of conduct is due from us, and that, failing its performance, it is just, or due from us, that we should suffer. Now in virtue of a threefold relationship in which each one of us is created, we are in debt or under obligation to three parties—ourselves, our neighbours, and God—which three obligations the gospel of grace recognizes when it teaches us, in the language of the Apostle, to 'live soberly, righteously, and godly in this present world.'

First, we owe a debt to ourselves as God's stewards of the body, or animal nature, to keep it in temperance, soberness, and chastity; of the mind, or intellectual nature, to improve and cultivate it by every means in our power, in the knowledge of divine truth; in the line and for the purposes of our vocation; thirdly as stewards of the soul, or spiritual nature, to give its interests the pre-eminence and the first consideration, to make the mind its subordinate, and the body its instrument and its slave. This obligation to ourselves is repudiated by immoderate asceticism, which, in its extremer forms, aims, as in the Stoic and the Buddhist, at extirpating and crushing all the bodily and the natural instincts.

Secondly, we owe a debt to our neighbour—that we should 'live righteously'; we are under a natural obligation, arising from our brotherly relationship to him, to love him as ourselves, to respect his rank, his person, his affections, his property, his good name, his spiritual interests. The recluse, who shuts himself up from human society, that he personally may be out of harm's way, repudiates and refuses to acknowledge this debt.

Thirdly, and above all, we owe a debt to God—that we should 'live godly'; we are under a perpetual obligation, arising from our filial relationship to Him, to 'love the Lord our God with all our heart and with all our mind,' &c.; to improve in His service and to His glory all the talents with which He has entrusted us; to yield Him the fruits of His vineyard, that is, a substantial return for all the religious advantages and gracious influences which He bestows; to do the work of His service with our hands, to run on His errands with our feet, to admire His works of nature with our eyes, to listen to His word with our ears, to sing His praises with our tongue, so that each of our members may yield to Him some homage. The mere moralist, who, while he admits that man is subject to moral laws which he cannot violate with impunity, at the same time ignores or denies the personality of God, and consequently the claims arising out of His relationship to us, repudiates and refuses to recognize this obligation. And failing to discharge these debts, or any of them, our consciences assure us that the failure should be met by a corresponding punishment—that we 'ought' to suffer. They instinctively recognize God as a judge who, in virtue of the purity and uprightness of His character, cannot clear the guilty.

But now the figure of a debt having been explained, what is the special instructiveness of it? What points does it bring out respecting sin, which, but for this representation of it, we might have missed? This chiefly, that it gives such a prominence to sins of omission—a prominence foreign indeed to our habits of thought, but altogether in harmony with the teaching of God's Word. If sins had gone under no other name than 'sins,' we might have understood by them nothing but positive wrongs, vices, injuries inflicted upon society, insults offered to God, and so forth. But when sins are spoken of as unpaid debts, how different an aspect does the case assume! A debt is something not rendered which ought to have been rendered. I do not incur a debt to a man when I assault him and break one of his limbs, nor when I calumniate him and take away his character, nor even when I take his property from him by violence or fraud. The 'being in debt' to a man means, not that I do anything to him which I should not, but that I leave undone what I should do to him, namely, the repayment of his money. And thus the constant thinking of sin under the image of a debt brings out, more strongly than any other phraseology could do, the omissory side of sin—that, in its main aspect, sin is the non-payment of something inherently and essentially due; the non-payment to God of love and glory, to man of sympathy and brotherly kindness. And exactly in accordance with the estimate of sin, which this phraseology leads us to form, will be the Divine Judge's sentence upon sinners at the last day. What He will comment upon in that sentence, and set before them, when it is now too late to amend their error, will be the neglect of duty to Him and to their brethren, which there has been in their wrong-doing; the waste of time, the non-improvement of talents, the ignoring of claims, the non-recognition of neighbours as neighbours, the non-exhibition of sympathies—'I was an hungred, and ye gave Me no meat: I was thirsty, and ye gave Me no drink: I was a stranger, and ye took Me not in: naked, and ye clothed Me not: sick, and in prison, and ye visited Me not. . . . Inasmuch as ye did it not to one of the least of these, ye did it not to Me' (St. Matt. xxv. 42, 43, 45).

It opens a wide field of thought on the nature of sin to regard every form of it in the light in which our Lord here instructs us to regard it— as the non-payment of something intrinsically due from us either to God, our neighbours, or ourselves.

Observe, once more (because this is essential to the right understanding of the petition before us), that the debts, for whose remission we petition, are daily incurred debts. We may say, generally, that each petition of the Lord's Prayer is to be understood in the light of all that has preceded it, and is bound up in the body of thought which has already been accumulated. So here; 'Give us day by day our daily bread, and,' *concurrently with bread* (that is, day by day also), 'give us pardon.' Again, the 'Our Father,' with which the prayer begins, is a key-note which dominates the whole strain, and ever recurs in each clause of it; so that this petition is by no means to be understood as the voice of criminals condemned to death and imploring the judge to extend mercy to them, but as the voice of children running to their parent's knees before bedtime, burying their head in his lap, confessing that their conduct and temper during the day has been wrong, and seeking his forgiveness; 'Our Father, forgive us our debts.' The petition assumes, you will observe, that the petitioner has been placed in, and is realizing, his relationship to God as a reconciled child. He has a warrant and title to call God 'Father,' which no man has, or can have, except through the Sacrament of Baptism, 'wherein he was made ... the child of God'; and he has also the power and disposition to call God 'Father,' which no man has, or can have, except through faith; for 'Ye are all the children of God by faith in Christ Jesus' (Gal. iii. 26).

Our Lord speaks enigmatically to St. Peter of a twofold washing—one of the entire person, another of the feet. 'He that is washed' (i.e. he whose whole person is bathed) 'needeth not save to wash his feet, but is clean every whit.' That is to say, there is one great spiritual cleansing when a heathen is turned from darkness to light, and is washed, sanctified, and justified in the laver of regeneration by baptism. He, upon whom this process has passed, 'needeth not save to wash his feet,' i.e. to wipe off the dust and soil which is necessarily contracted by a single day's walk in this naughty world. When we seek from 'Our Father, which is in heaven,' the forgiveness of our sins, it is this wiping off of the daily dust and soil which we solicit, so that our consciences may be kept in a state of habitual brightness and clearness, and that the rust, which the foul breath of this world is apt to form upon them, may be cleared away as soon as it begins to accumulate. Watchfulness, therefore, and daily self-examination are among the duties which this petition suggests; for how is the rust to be detected, except by means of these exercises? But the petition speaks of comfort, of large and precious comfort, as well as of duty. For it shows clearly, as St. Chrysostom says, that 'even after the laver [of regeneration] the profit of repentance is not taken away.' Must not He who, in framing this holy prayer, inserted a petition for the forgiveness of daily sins, have contemplated our falling into such sins, through the frailty of our nature? Must He not have foreseen that the children of God would have need to come to their Father's feet evening after evening, and pour out a confession of lapses of the tongue and lapses of the temper, and sometimes even of more serious falls incurred through forgetfulness of God? So in this petition He provides a remedy for these lapses, and teaches us to seek a fresh outflow of compassion from our Father's fatherly heart, to obliterate them all.

It would be to omit a consideration all essential to the right understanding of the subject if it were not pointed out that it is in virtue of Christ's having, while on earth, discharged all our debts, that God now remits them. Christ is the second Adam—the second and better representative of our race. And standing, not for

Himself, but for us, in the nature common to us all, He as man discharged every claim of obedience, devotion, love, sympathy, which either God or man had upon Him. Moreover, while perfectly exempt from sin both in His flesh and His spirit, He implicated Himself in all the awful consequences of sin, and submitted in body and mind to its severest penalty, thus discharging the debt of suffering, as He had already discharged the debt of obedience. But while we may scripturally and rightly look at our Lord's work for us under this image, let us beware of pressing (as some do) so unduly hard upon the image as to suppose that it will hold good in every point. There is one point in which it does not hold good, and which shows that God, while He employs it, is accommodating His inscrutable ways to our feeble forms of thought and expression. The point is this. Christ, in the payment of our debt, is not a person acting independently of God, or not in concert with the Father. To suppose anything like this is to strain a figurative expression beyond what it will bear. It was of the free mercy and pure grace of God that Christ was sent to pay our debts; the discharge of them was not more an act of grace on the Son's part than an act of love on the Father's. Now, in the earthly transaction, which is made a figure of this, no man ever heard of a creditor's providing, at great cost to himself, the payment of a debtor's debt by some third person. If the earthly creditor pities and wishes to relieve the debtor, he simply remits the debt. Here therefore the earthly image breaks down beneath the burden of the heavenly truth. And it is to our comfort that it should break down; for while it expresses sufficiently the love of Christ, who bore our sins in His own body on the tree, it fails to express the love of God, who gave up His Son out of His bosom, thus to bear our sins, and herein gives the glorious pledge that He will do for us all that is further necessary for our holiness and happiness: 'He that spared not His own Son, but delivered Him up for us all, how shall He not with Him also freely give us all things?' (Rom. viii. 32). As often as we say, 'Forgive us our trespasses,' let us open our hearts to that self-sacrificing love of God, as a sunflower opens its bosom to the sun; let us believe in its freeness, in its universality, in its moral power, and we shall find that it will not only obliterate our sins, but draw us sweetly and efficaciously out of them.

CHAPTER XIII

AS WE FORGIVE OUR DEBTORS

THE two sections (or, as we may call them, the two tables) of the Lord's Prayer correspond very exactly to one another. In each of these sections, one of the petitions has a modifying clause annexed to it by the particle 'as.' In the first section, we pray that God's will may be done in earth, '*as* it is in heaven.' In the second section, we pray that He would forgive us our trespasses, '*as* we forgive them that trespass against us.' There is an evident parallelism in the structure of the first and second parts of the Prayer, which is curious and interesting. But the parallelism does not extend to the thought which is expressed by the words. The 'as' in the first section of the Prayer does not mean the same as the 'as' now before us in its second section. In the clause, 'Thy will be done in earth as it is in heaven,' the 'as' means according to the model of. We pray that men upon earth may imitate, and take as their model, the fervour, alacrity, and zeal with which the blessed angels of heaven execute God's behests. But in the corresponding clause, 'As we forgive our debtors,' we surely do not implore God to make our forgiveness of the sins of others His model in forgiving us. 'God forbid,' says good Bishop Andrewes, that He should no otherwise forgive us than we forgive our brethren.' The 'as' here merely expresses the condition, on which we trust that God will graciously extend His forgiveness to ourselves. And that this is indeed the meaning of the clause is evident from the words in which St. Luke couches the idea, and which are different from the words in St. Matthew: 'For we also forgive every one that is indebted to us.' The 'for' is only another way of stating the 'as.' And the 'for' can only mean that we entreat God to forgive us, in consideration of our complying with the condition of pardon, which He Himself has laid down, viz. that we shall forgive others.

We have here a good instance of the importance of examining carefully the different phrases in which Holy Scripture conveys an idea. One of these phrases will often explain and guard another; and perhaps correct an erroneous inference, which might have been drawn from the other phrase, had it stóod alone.

That the clause at which we have now arrived is one of peculiar importance is evident from the unique emphasis which the giver of the Prayer laid on it. It is the only clause upon which He commented after His first giving of the Prayer; thus drawing special attention to it, as if it were the most noticeable point in the whole formula: 'For if ye forgive men their trespasses, your heavenly Father will also forgive you: but if ye forgive not men their trespasses, neither will your Father forgive your trespasses' (St. Matt. vi. 14, 15).

But this is by no means the only evidence of our Lord attaching special weight to the clause. At a later period of His ministry, He devoted a parable to the illustration of the idea which it conveys. The parable of the Unmerciful Servant graphically represents the doom of the unforgiving Christian, and brings out in strong relief a point, obvious indeed, but not expressly noticed in the Prayer; namely, the enormous disproportion between our debts to one another, and those which we all owe to God, the one being represented as 'an hundred pence' (something short of four pounds in our money), the other as 10,000 talents (something considerably over a million and a half).

When we consider that our obligations to God extend over every waking moment of our lives; that the smallest deviation of the heart from His love, and of the will from the intention of serving and glorifying Him, constitutes an unfulfilled obligation, for which punishment is due; that, moreover, our obligations to our neighbours and to ourselves are all of them in their higher aspect obligations to God; and that even 'a just' (i.e. a righteous and a spiritual man) 'falleth seven times a day' (Prov. xxiv. 16), (seven here being used, as so often in Holy Scripture, for a perfect number); while, on the other hand, the offences which pass between us and our neighbours, the injuries which they do to us, and the enmities which estrange us from them, are the exception, not the rule, of daily life, this enormous disproportion will not at all surprise us; evidently the aggregate of all the wrongs ever done to us by suspicion, word, or deed, can bear no comparison whatever with the extent of our own unfulfilled obligations to God. Since, then, our blessed Lord has called our attention so very pointedly to this particular clause, we must give the more heed to it, and study to understand the ground of it, and more and more to imbibe its spirit.

First; let us be very clear as to what a condition of Divine forgiveness means. The condition of God's forgiveness is something altogether distinct from its meritorious ground. To distinguish between the two by an illustration, we may suppose that a person imprisoned for debt is entitled to be discharged by the payment of the debt in full by another person, but yet is discharged on the express understanding that he will not exact from others any sums which may be due to himself. The understanding is only the condition of his discharge; it is the payment of his debt which constitutes his legal title to it, and which may be called its meritorious ground. The single meritorious ground of our forgiveness is, as was explained in the last chapter, the work of Christ. Standing for us in the nature common to all as our representative, He discharged in full all our obligations, whether they be obligations to obey or obligations to suffer. And on this meritorious ground God remits to us our debt; but at the same time not without annexing a condition, with which we must comply. And the condition of our enjoying remission, and the other blessings which follow in its train, is that we shall extend to others the mercy which we have ourselves received.

That this condition should make its appearance in the model prayer of the Christian is most reasonable. For this model prayer was intended to indicate, not only the blessings which we should ask of God, but the spirit in which we must ask them, if we would gain them. On a memorable occasion our Lord Himself exhibited the spirit in which men should pray, if they would fetch down from heaven the blessings they solicit. He said it must be a spirit of faith, and also a spirit of forgiving love. He had just uttered against the barren fig-tree a prayer of malediction: 'No man eat fruit of thee hereafter for ever' (St. Mark xi. 14). The prayer had taken effect instantaneously; and the disciples when passing the fig-tree next morning remark in surprise the speedy accomplishment of their Master's words; 'How soon is the fig-tree withered away!' Jesus proceeds to instruct them (most appositely to the phenomenon on which their thoughts were dwelling) as to the conditions on which their words of prayer should be, as His had been, words of power. The first of these conditions was, that they should pray in faith: 'Have faith in God,' faith in His word of promise, in His willingness to give, in His ability to give, and therefore in the certainty of His giving such things as it is good for us to have. Now this faith in God is implied in every word of the first part of the Lord's Prayer. We cannot sincerely call God 'Father,' nor pray that 'His name may be hallowed,' nor that 'His kingdom may come,' nor that 'His will may be done,'—our hearts cannot echo these phrases and petitions without 'faith in God.'

But there is a second, and equally important, condition of success in prayer, which our Lord proceeded to point out: 'And when ye stand praying, forgive, if ye have ought against any: that your Father also which is in heaven may forgive you your trespasses. But if ye do not forgive, neither will your Father which is in heaven forgive your trespasses.' The forgiveness of those who are indebted to us; the prayer for those who have done us an ill turn; the not insisting upon claims upon which strictly we might insist; the remitting freely part of the respect or privileges which are rightfully our due—this, if it be sincere, and not professed or hypocritical, cannot flow from any motive but love. Forgiveness is love's highest exercise both in God and in man. God's bounty to His creatures, His liberality in providing them with sustenance and outward comforts, is by no means the highest or most convincing evidence of His love for us. 'Scarcely for a righteous man will one die: yet peradventure for a good man some would even dare to die. But God commendeth His love toward us, in that, while we were yet sinners, Christ died for us' (Rom. v. 7, 8). The highest evidence of God's love is His making over His Son to a cruel death for a world in arms against Himself. This gift showed conclusively a longing on our heavenly Father's part to be reconciled to the worst and vilest of those who had rebelled against Him. It is therefore in this particular act of love, 'the forgiveness of sins,' that this Divine Prayer calls upon us to imitate Him, who 'maketh His sun to shine upon the evil and the good, and sendeth rain on the just and on the unjust' (St. Matt. v. 45).

Moreover, this forgiveness of offences is, and is felt to be, the most supernatural of all virtues. The moment our thoughts turn to it, we must acknowledge that Nature is not competent to this achievement. To certain exercises of love Nature is more or less competent, though even here she derives a quickening and a stimulus from grace. Nature may dispose us to relieve abject distress, or to show generosity to a completely crushed and vanquished foe. But to deal indulgently with one who advisedly passes a slight upon us, or injures our reputation, or stands in the way of our advancement, or thwarts our fondest wishes, this is instinctively felt to be far above the standard of natural virtue. And when the duty of forgiving an enemy, however often he may have offended us, was pressed upon the disciples by their Divine Lord, the Apostles, in the feeling that for compliance with this precept they needed an extraordinary supply of the principle which lifts man above the things that are seen, said unto the Lord, 'Increase our faith.' By far the hardest exercise of love is to forgive those who have offended us; and therefore our Lord selects this rather than any other exercise, in order more conclusively to indicate the presence of the spirit of love in the petitioner.

Here again, let us admire the high standard which this Prayer contemplates in those who use it. It assumes that the heart of the petitioner is set, first and before all things else, on the hallowing of God's name and the advancement of His kingdom. It assumes also that his heart is so softened by the exercise of God's pardoning mercy towards himself, that he cannot but extend the same mercy to others. Alas! how often have we allowed ourselves to repeat the words of the Prayer, without the germ of either of these dispositions! And how much therefore have we to answer for in the way of taking God's name in vain in our prayers! How often, when on our knees before Him, have we expressed sentiments to which our hearts were strangers! And as in saying, 'Thy kingdom come,' when there was in us no preparedness for its coming, we have virtually asked God to give us no more space for repentance; so in saying, 'Forgive us our trespasses, as we forgive them that trespass against us,' we have often virtually asked him to stint His large and liberal measure of forgiveness, and to receive our penitence coldly and with nice calculations of its genuineness and depth.

But before we part with this clause, we must attempt to reach the real and hidden ground of this condition, 'As we forgive our debtors.' It is not a condition arbitrarily imposed; God does not arbitrarily lay any restrictions upon His bounty, although we may so represent the matter to ourselves. Rather the condition is inherent in the constitution of our nature, which is not fundamentally altered by the Gospel; for to alter it fundamentally would be to construct a new creature, instead of restoring the old one. The human heart, then, is so framed that it cannot open towards God to receive His mercy, without at the same time opening towards man, and even towards injurious and offending man, to give him welcome. It may seem theoretically possible to receive forgiveness from our heavenly Father, without extending it to our earthly brethren; but it is not practically feasible. The two avenues of the heart, its avenue towards God and its avenue towards man, open, as it were, and close with one and the same door. It is not merely true that a man will not receive forgiveness from God who does not extend it to his neighbour, but rather he *cannot* receive it. God may be ready and longing to forgive; but the avenue of the heart, through which alone forgiveness can be poured into it, is not opened. We may take an illustration from a somewhat analogous feature in the constitution of the human mind. Susceptibility to the beauty of a work of art or of a poem carries with it more or less a desire and an endeavour to produce poetry, to utter oneself in the form of poetry. The receptive faculty is also more or less a constructive and productive faculty; so that the soul, into which poetry finds a ready entrance, will occasionally seek to pour itself forth in poetry. Similarly in the case before us, love is a thing which we cannot embrace without extending love to others. In that softening of the soul which is the result of realizing the Divine love in Christ, it is nothing less than impossible, to harbour a grudge against our neighbour. And, therefore, if a grudge were harboured by any soul, this would conclusively show that that soul is not really softened, has never been a recipient of God's pardoning mercy, however freely that mercy may have been proffered to it.

When the heart has been thoroughly penetrated with God's love to ourselves, it is in no humour to make terms with others, to stand upon rights and claims with them, or to measure the amount of forgiveness which it deals forth to them. It cannot possibly take up the mental attitude indicated in that question put by St. Peter to the Master, 'Lord, how oft shall my brother sin against me, and I forgive him? till seven times?' (St. Matt. xviii. 21.) God's pardon is measureless; and accordingly any *measure* of forgiveness to those whose offences against ourselves have been so much less, is felt to be intolerable. God's generosity experienced by ourselves has made additional room in our hearts, and our offending brethren are at once received into that room. The question is, how much love we can show them; not how little we may show them, consistently with our own safety. Any attempt to limit, or dole out by measure, the forgiveness we extend to others, would only show that we have no real appreciation of God's love to ourselves; for this Love is expressly said to include the forgetting of past sins: 'Their sins and their iniquities will I remember no more,' 'Thou wilt cast all their sins into the depths of the sea.' At any rate, if we have not a power of obliteration over our memory, we can habitually do all in our power to banish from our mind every trace of resentment; if, on principle, we never allow our thoughts to dwell on a slight or an insult (for the dwelling on it ever so little is sure to magnify its proportions); if we perseveringly pray for those who have offended or injured us, and seize gladly every opportunity of showing them kindness; if our wills be right in this matter, and consistently refuse to give a hearing to the feelings of our corrupt nature; with what comfortable assurance of receiving it may we solicit from God the remission of our own sins! For can we suppose that He will be less generous and merciful to us than we are to our neighbours? Is it not certain that for every debt we find grace from Him to remit, He will remit ten thousand; and that for every opening of our sympathies

As we Forgive our Debtors 237

towards an offending brother, He will pour out upon us such treasures of Divine affection that we shall not have room to receive them? 'What is my hope?' says good Bishop Andrewes in a most urgent and pathetic appeal to the Saviour for pardon. 'It is that Thou even unto seventy times seven dost extend Thy mercy. For this is the measure which Thou hast commended to us. Hast Thou commended it to us that we should exercise it amongst ourselves, but that Thou Thyself shouldest not exercise the same? Yea, Thou wilt exercise it and much more. Far be it from Thee that Thou shouldest require more perfection to be in us than is in Thyself; that Thou shouldest require us to forgive unto seventy times seven, but Thyself shouldest be unwilling to do so. For Thy mercy surpasseth ours as far as Thou Thyself surpasseth us.'

Yes, this forgetting as well as forgiving love of our God is to be our model in dealing out forgiveness to our offending brethren. 'It is an arduous and difficult requirement,' you will say, 'if not in the majority of cases, at least where the wrong done has been deliberate, and evidently of malice prepense, and is of a kind which not only damages us externally, but also wounds the feelings.' Let us see whether another consideration, drawn from that love of God which is to be our model, may not, when calmly pondered, somewhat reduce the proportions of the difficulty. We are to love as God loves, to forgive as our heavenly Father forgives. Our mind in the matter is to be framed upon His. But while God loves the worst sinners tenderly, while the measure of His love to them is nothing less than the gift of His Son out of His bosom for them and to them, still He hates their sins, so much so that unless they were delivered from the guilt of those sins by His Son's blood, and from the power of them by His Son's grace, He could not accept them. Assuredly He cannot require us to love what He Himself hates. It is the person of mine enemy that I am required to love, not his wrong or his wrongdoing. And so St. Augustine very beautifully teaches us to distinguish, as the Divine Love does, between the sinner and the sin.

' It is not the human nature [in thine enemy] that is at enmity with thee, but his sin. If he had no evil, he would not be thine enemy. Wish him well, then, that he may end his ill, and he will be thine enemy no longer.'

CHAPTER XIV

AND LEAD US NOT INTO TEMPTATION

When our Lord found in the Temple the man to whom He had restored the use of his limbs at the Pool of Bethesda, He gave him this salutary warning: 'Behold, thou art made whole: sin no more, lest a worse thing come unto thee' (St. John v. 14). And the Apostle St. Peter, echoing what his Master had once said respecting the return of the evil spirit, with seven other spirits more wicked than himself, into the man from whom he had been temporarily cast out, says of certain false teachers of his time, 'For if after they have escaped the pollutions of the world through the knowledge of the Lord and Saviour Jesus Christ, they are

And Lead us not into Temptation

again entangled therein, and overcome, the latter end is worse with them than the beginning... But it is happened unto them according to the true proverb, The dog is turned to his own vomit again; and the sow that was washed to her wallowing in the mire' (2 St. Peter ii. 20, 22).

In these and similar passages we find the significance of the 'and,' which links together 'Lead us not into temptation' with 'Forgive us our trespasses.' Our souls have been healed by the precious balm of Christ's blood, by the blessed restorative of God's pardon; we have escaped from our pollutions of heart and life; the unclean spirit has taken his departure, exorcised by the spell of God's great love. Now, therefore, our care must be to sin no more: we must fortify ourselves against the return of the evil spirit to our heart; we must look to it that we do not, after being washed in the Blood of Christ, turn again to our wallowing in the mire of sin (p. 17).

We shall appreciate this petition more fully, and repeat it more heartily, if we consider how apt the same sins and faults of character are to recur day after day with us; how each evening's self-examination brings to light much the same slips of temper and the tongue, much the same omissions of devotion, much the same waste of time, much the same wandering of the thoughts in forbidden directions, as that of yesterday; so that, alas! upon the whole we seem to make but little way. It should not be so, our consciences tell us. He who confesses sins, without earnestly striving against them, has good reason to fear that his confession has not been an honest one. We profess before God, evening after evening, that we deplore the faults by which we have been that day overtaken. But do we deplore them if we make no effort to avoid them? And such an effort can only be successful if made under God's direction and in His strength. Reasonably, therefore, we pray, after making mention of sins past, for God's help against sins future: 'Forgive us our trespasses, AND lead us not into temptation.'

There are two ways of contemplating future trials of our Christian principle. The first is exemplified in St. Peter. Assured of his own sincere attachment to his Master, and conscious of the warmth of his feelings, he challenged temptation, and asked to have his affection put to the proof: 'Lord, I am ready to go with Thee, both into prison, and to death' (St. Luke xxii. 33). Observe that, in thus expressing himself, he did not foresee the exact danger he would have to meet; he was probably thinking of another form of danger, against which his own heart told him he at all events was proof. He thought of having to fight for Christ with the arms of flesh, and, if his sword was beaten down, of being captured and imprisoned in our Lord's company. And had this been the trial in store for him, there can be little doubt that he would have braved it nobly. He showed his perfect willingness to abide a trial of that sort by drawing his sword, and striking the servant of the high priest. He expected, doubtless, that this would have been the signal for the swords of the apprehending party to leap from their scabbards, and for a skirmish to ensue between them and the Apostles, in which he would no doubt, under the impulse of enthusiastic admiration for our Lord, have acquitted himself as a brave man. But the issue was far different. Not a blade was raised to meet his. Our Lord was not going to use, nor to allow His followers to use, violence. He bids Peter (St. Matt. xxvi. 52) 'put up again' his 'sword into his place,' and repairs, by an exertion of miraculous power, the mischief which that sword had done. And now appeared the other form of temptation, for which Peter was all unprepared—not the form which had shown itself to him in the foreground, and which he felt that he could easily conquer, but the form which was lying in ambush for him. Many a man has been found ready to march up to the cannon's mouth in the cause of his country, who would be quite unable to bear the brunt of contempt and ridicule. Peter would have fought to the death by the side of Messiah, and would have gloried in doing so; but to be pointed at by the finger of scorn among the high priest's servants, to be despised of men as the follower and associate of the Galilaean, who claimed to be Messiah, and yet seemed as if He could not lift a finger to help Himself out of His own difficulties,—this was a trial which could only be met in the strength of grace, not of natural resolution; and accordingly Peter, who had entrenched himself on natural resolution, fell at once and shamefully, when it was brought to bear upon him.

The petition, 'Lead us not into temptation,' expresses a spirit the very opposite of that which challenges trial. He who in his morning prayer says this petition with his heart, realizing God's forgiveness of him, and conscious of acceptance with Him through the blood of the cross, while his heart glows with gratitude to his heavenly Father, and to his merciful Redeemer, for making him again welcome after so many falls, feels that he is going forth into a world which is everywhere a scene of temptation, and which offers perils both hidden and obvious at every turn, and that 'it is not in man that walketh to direct his steps' (Jer. x. 23) in such a world. He is a reconciled child indeed, and the sweet sense of reconciliation is shed abroad in his heart 'by the Holy Ghost which is given unto him' (see Rom. v. 5). But he is profoundly suspicious of the world; profoundly diffident of himself. His enemies are versed in spiritual warfare; they succeed oftener by ambush or stratagem than by direct assault. He cannot see them; he cannot detect where they are driving their mines, or under what covert they are concealing their forces. He remembers that even in our first parents' state of innocence, before sin had entered their nature and given it a bias towards evil, Satan proved more than a match for them; in his heart there is 'the infection of nature' which 'doth remain yea in them that are regenerated,' and which is ever ready to correspond with the enemy; how shall he ever hope to stand against Satan in his own wisdom or strength? He would therefore, feeling himself 'to be set in the midst of so many and great dangers, that by reason of the frailty of' his 'nature' he 'cannot always stand upright,' rather decline the contest, if it be God's will, than venture into it. At all events, however assured at present of pardon and Divine favour, his prayer shall never run in the form of a challenge; he will never say in the spirit of Goliath, 'I defy the armies of' the evil ones 'this day' (1 Sam. xvii. 10); but rather, in the words of Goliath's despised and unarmed adversary, 'I come to thee in the name of the Lord of Hosts, the God of the armies of Israel' (1 Sam. xvii. 45). 'Our Father which art in heaven, lead us not into temptation.'

'Lead us not into temptation.' God is here regarded as the authorizer, rather than the author, of temptation or of trial (for the word might equally well, if not better, be so rendered). Of course there is a certain sense in which reason, reverence, and Holy Scripture assure us that God cannot be its author: 'Let no man say when he is tempted, I am tempted of God: for God cannot be tempted with evil, neither tempteth He any man' (James i. 13). If by temptation be meant the infusion of a bad thought into the mind, the instilment of an evil suggestion, or the stirring up and quickening into a flame the embers of our natural corruption, then God can never tempt directly; temptation in this sense must be due exclusively to agents at enmity with God, viz. the world and the devil. But it should be observed that in this glorious prayer our point of sight is raised above all created agency to Him, by whose permission at least all creatures must act, even when they act in contravention to His will. There is a great truth underlying this reference of all things to God, even those which are in opposition to Him. But let us first consider the primary idea of the Prayer. God may be said to 'bring' or 'lead' men (the first word is a more exact translation than the second) into trial or temptation in one of three ways: firstly, by the agency of His providence; secondly, by His permission; thirdly, by the withdrawal of grace.

First, *by the agency of His providence*. It will not be denied that the circumstances in which we find ourselves placed, are appointed by, and under the control of, Divine Providence. By the arrangements of this Providence, one man is born to wealth and large property, another in the condition of a peasant; one man receives high mental culture, another remains all his life in ignorance of any but the humblest rudiments of learning; one person is entrusted with the administration of an empire, another with that of a small household; one man is surrounded from his earliest youth by religious, another by irreligious, associations. It is a great truth, and one which must be carefully borne in mind in forming an estimate of temptations, that all circumstances without exception have their peculiar trials, so that a change of position in life is never at any time an exemption from trial, but only the exchange of one form of trial for another. And this being the case, it might be supposed that circumstances were in this point of view indifferent to men, and that whether God should bring us into one set of circumstances or another, it really would not make much difference, since He never brings us into any which are exempt from trial. But it must be remembered that, while all circumstances are beset with temptations, all temptations are not equally forcible to all characters, nor even to the same characters at all times. A man who is not much open to temptations from the flesh—a man of cold, phlegmatic temperament and spare diet—may be easily accessible to the snares of intellectual pride; in which case to place him in a position where he has no leisure, or means, or opportunity to study, would be to shield him from temptation; and, on the other hand, to give him books, and education, and leisure, and none but himself to provide for, would be to bring him into temptation. And, again, the temptations which for the most part beset us all in youth—clamorous passions, vehement longings to choose for ourselves in life, love of gaiety and dissipation—all in the order of Nature, or (to speak more accurately) in the order of God's Providence, relax their grasp in later years. Again, under ordinary circumstances a person may be entirely free from temptations to dishonesty and murmuring; but let his property become insecure, or a dear friend, intimately associated with him, be taken from his side, and the temptation springs up in an instant. So that the petition, 'Lead us not into temptation,' may be, under our present view of it, paraphrased thus: 'Place me not, O God, in circumstances which either my peculiar natural temperament, or my

And Lead us not into Temptation 251

age, or some unexpected turn of fortune will make severely trying to me.'

The considerateness of God in not bringing His children into temptation finds a beautiful and lively illustration in one of His dealings with His ancient people. 'And it came to pass, when Pharaoh had let the people go, that God led them not through the way of the land of the Philistines, although that was near; for God said, Lest peradventure the people repent when they see war, and they return to Egypt: but God led the people about, through the way of the wilderness of the Red Sea' (Exod. xiii. 17). The Israelites had been for generations a nation of serfs; courage and spirit had been trodden out of their hearts by Egyptian oppression. What they longed for was an easy life in servitude among the flesh-pots; they had no mind for the risks and perils involved in striking a bold stroke for freedom. To have led them therefore, just at the moment of their emancipation, through the land of the Philistines, amidst frowning fortresses and sallying foes, would have been a grievous discouragement, and God would season them a little by His gracious discipline in the wilderness before He submits them to a trial which, under their circumstances, would have been so fierce; He would not appal them by the sight of fortresses and lances and masterful men, while the associations of serfdom are fresh upon them, while they are weak, timid, and unnerved. In His fatherly considerateness for their circumstances, He will not lead them into temptation.

Secondly, God leads us into temptation when He gives licence to the devil, and, under certain restrictions, permits him to tempt us. Even these temptations are ascribed to God, because they are immediately and supremely under His control. And when our Saviour teaches us to pray thus: 'Lead us not into temptation,' rather than thus: 'Do not allow the devil to tempt us,' He mercifully consoles and strengthens our hearts by hiding the created agency which there is behind the temptation, and pointing us to the Infinite Power, Wisdom, and Love which appoints, permits, presides over, and controls the temptation. He takes no express notice

And Lead us not into Temptation 253

of the devil, who after all is only an instrument, and reminds us that 'Our Father, who is in heaven,' is ruling still, has not for a single moment let the reins of administration slip out of His hands. Yes! the weakest Christian may address to Satan the same language which his dear Lord addressed to Pilate, 'Thou couldest have no power at all against Me, except it were given thee from above' (St. John xix. 11). By thus dealing even with the most manifestly Satanic temptations, by reflecting that Satan is bridled and cannot stir without God's giving him a signal, he may nerve himself for the conflict and gather strength to overcome.

It should be added here that God's licence for Satanic temptations is of two kinds, and for two different issues. Sometimes the licence is given for action upon a good man, for the trial and approval of his faith and his patience; sometimes (it is an awful truth; but it is scriptural, and we must not conceal it) upon a bad man, to seal his doom and sweep him headlong out of life into 'his own place.' The story of good Job furnishes an instance of the first kind of licence. Satan obtains from God permission to assault successively Job's cattle, Job's servants, Job's children, and Job's health. Stripped of all things, and smarting under the wrongful reproaches of his friends, the servant of God, nevertheless, in the main, though not without distressing misgivings and much self-justification, speaks of God 'the things that are right.' Then, when the faith and patience of Job have been approved, and he himself humbled in the dust and taught many valuable lessons, He who 'doth not afflict willingly, nor grieve the children of men' (Lam. iii. 33), restored to him all his prosperity in double splendour.

An instance of a licence for a final assault of Satanic power upon a bad man may be found in the history of Ahab. God is seen by Micaiah in a vision, surrounded by His heavenly court. 'And the Lord said, Who shall persuade Ahab, that he may go up and fall at Ramoth-Gilead? And one said on this manner, and another said on that manner. And there came forth a spirit, and stood before the Lord, and said, I will persuade him. And the Lord said unto him,

And Lead us not into Temptation 255

Wherewith? And he said, I will go forth, and I will be a lying spirit in the mouth of all his prophets. And he said, Thou shalt persuade him, and prevail also: go forth, and do so' (1 Kings xxii. 20-22).

And so, in the plain unfigurative language of St. Paul, God sent unto this wicked prince a 'strong delusion, that' he 'should believe a lie' (2 Thess. ii. 11) and perish in the belief of it. And in the minds of all those who believe the Scriptures to be the Word of God, there can be no doubt that when a man, after a long course of dishonesty, and a vain struggle to keep up appearances, has made shipwreck of the worldly fortunes of himself and his family; or, after a long course of intemperance, has made shipwreck of his health, and become the prey of nervous irritation and debility; Satan is often, as a final temptation, permitted to be in that man 'a lying spirit'; and a voice whispers to him that life indeed is full of evils, but in the grave there is repose and peace and escape from all troubles; and, under this 'strong delusion,' he adjusts the halter round his neck, or places the pistol to his brain, or smears the deadly poison upon his tongue, and rushes, not upon eternal sleep of unconsciousness (as he had vainly dreamed), but upon eternal ruin. We all, even the best and holiest among us, stand purely and merely upon grace. Our natural instincts are as corrupt, as tainted at the spring, as those of the prodigal or the suicide-drunkard. How earnestly should we therefore pray, in contemplation of their awful doom, 'Our Father which art in heaven' . . . 'Lead us not into temptation'! Give us not over for our sins to a 'lying spirit.' Send not upon us a 'strong delusion' that we should believe a lie.

Thirdly, the last method by which God leads us into temptation is by the subtraction or withdrawal of His Holy Spirit. The great scriptural example (and these concrete examples enable us to apprehend the truth in a far more lively manner than the most exact and fullest abstract description) is Hezekiah. This excellent and devout prince allowed himself to be puffed up by the extraordinary favours which God had shown him, in miraculously protecting his city and prolonging his life. 'Who so great a prince as I,' thought Hezekiah, 'from whose ramparts God repels the invading host of the Assyrians, and in whose behalf He rolls back the forward march of Time, and makes the sun return ten degrees, by which degrees it was gone down?' So Hezekiah, for the improvement of his own spiritual character, for his own perfecting in holiness, must be taught that he is nothing apart from God, that he stands wholly and merely, like all other saints, on the free grace of God. So we read, 'In the business of the ambassadors of the princes of Babylon, who sent unto him to inquire of the wonder that was done in the land, God left him, to try him, that He might know all that was in his heart' (2 Chron. xxxii. 31).

'God left him,' and the result was an outbreak of vanity in the presence of the King of Babylon's ambassadors. Hezekiah conducted them with much self-gratulation over his treasuries and his arsenals, and received from them doubtless the compliments of a hollow flattery. Alas! the spectacle awaked not less of cupidity than of admiration in these foreigners; and Isaiah was commissioned to predict that the treasures, of which the king was so vain, should be carried as spoil to Babylon, and that his children should accompany them into a state of degrading servitude.

God's proving us, by the withdrawal of His Holy Spirit, 'that He may know what is in our hearts' is of course said of Him after the manner of men. 'All that is in our hearts,' even the first springs of thought and will, are to Him 'naked and opened' from the very first; but it is His purpose to make it apparent to ourselves for our humiliation, and 'to men and angels,' under whose eyes we are running our race, so that it may be acknowledged that in man, as he is by nature, there is no good thing, and that salvation is wholly by grace.

But we must endeavour to enter a little more deeply into the real ground of temptation being ascribed in this Prayer supremely to God. The liability, then, of rational creatures to temptation runs up ultimately into the Supreme Will, which ordained that there should be such creatures. It might have pleased God to endow no creatures whatsoever with free will and conscience—in a word, to have no other creatures than brute animals, which obey Him by instinct, and material objects, which obey Him by natural laws. But 'it was more worthy of God,' says Bishop Butler (and of all his great sayings it is one of the greatest), 'to create beings capable of loving Him, and of choosing His service out of love, than to make all things in the universe mere echoes of His own will, mere machines worked by the action of His own hand.' But then the capability of serving God freely out of love involves a capability of refusing such service upon certain inducements held out to the creature from other quarters. These inducements are called temptations. Some creatures fall under temptations. Failure in many cases is incidental to God's plan, is necessarily involved in the creature's having that highest, most solemn, most awful gift of free will. But many stand and conquer, and those who stand are not only approved and crowned, but also forwarded and matured in character, as they could not have been by anything short of so painful and, in many respects, humbling a discipline. To refer, then, to God as supremely the author of temptation is to recognize Him as the Creator, by His own and gracious will, of a universe in which there is not mere mechanical and chemical action, not mere natural laws, not mere unreasoning instinct, but also moral agency and probation of creatures, with all the tremendous issues which such agency and probation involve. Not to be at peace, but to overcome, as Christ overcame temptation, is the true aim of His members.

The practical lessons to be drawn from the subject are, first, that we should unite watchfulness against temptation with prayer in the prospect of it. Our Lord, it must be remembered, supplemented on another occasion the petition before us. He could not introduce watchfulness otherwise than by implication into His Prayer, because watchfulness is rather a duty of man, not a grace of God. But in precept He associated watchfulness with prayer as a preservative against temptation's power. 'Watch,' said He, 'and pray, that ye enter not into temptation' (St. Matt. xxvi. 41). And He said it at a period when His human mind was in extreme tension on the subject of trial; for it was in the very midst of His own sore trial in the garden that He gave this warning to sleeping disciples. The recurrence of old faults, which (as already noticed) is so painful an experience in the spiritual life of many Christians, is due no doubt in great measure to their omitting to watch, as well as pray, against those faults. Their thoughts are all abroad; they maintain no self-collectedness; heedfulness of dangers they throw to the wind; they are not on the alert for the snares and assaults of the enemy, and therefore in those snares they are readily entrapped. To pray sincerely, 'Lead us not into temptation,' involves a will to watch against temptation.'

Secondly, the sincere utterance of this petition against temptation involves the not running into it of our own accord, and (since we pray for others as well as ourselves) the never throwing it in the way of others. Places, haunts, society, entertainments (innocent, perhaps, in the abstract and for others, but proved by experience to be spiritually mischievous to ourselves)—we must avoid them all if we would live in the spirit of this petition. No mockery can be conceived more shocking than that of perversely going whither we have deliberately asked God not to bring us. And how careful should we be to avoid the awful sin of putting a stumbling-block in our brother's way, of lowering his practical standard of duty by the felt influence of our example, nay, even of shocking his religious prejudices.

Men act as tempters to one another oftentimes, and Satan, whose legions of evil angels give him a kind of ubiquity, though of course neither he nor any other creature can be personally omnipresent, goes under the name of the tempter in Holy Scripture, as having human temptation, in all its varied forms, for his special province. But in the Lord's Prayer the agency both of evil men and of evil spirits is pretermitted and passed over *sub silentio* in the very petition which has temptation for its subject.

This entire exclusion of Satan from that part of the Prayer which deals with temptation, an exclusion which may at first sight surprise us, ought to be a help and a comfort to us in our warfare, teaching us that formidable as is the power of Satan, his strength is as nothing in comparison with the strength of the Almighty, who controls him, and holds him bitted and bridled, even when He suffers him to tempt.

There have been dark and impious heresies in the Church, which have acknowledged two co-ordinate principles of light and darkness, good and evil—two gods in rivalry one with another, of almost equal power. And though theoretically such absurdities are no longer maintained by Christians, they make a step in this direction, who, in a spirit of puritanical austerity, virtually recognize Satan not as the usurper, which he is, but as the rightful lord of the world, who has all human society and all human institutions for his province. It is not so. 'The earth is the Lord's, and the fullness thereof.' Human society is a creation of God's; human law is an ordinance of God's. And God is Light and Love; He is 'Our Father which is in heaven.'

The evil which is in the world is a usurpation and a tyranny; He has it under perfect control now—it is subserving His ends, even while it aims a blow at Him—and eventually He will cast it out. Hold His hand fast in your temptations, and you are perfectly safe. He 'will not suffer you to be tempted above that ye are able; but will with the temptation also make a way to escape, that ye may be able to bear it' (1 Cor. x. 13).

CHAPTER XV

BUT DELIVER US FROM EVIL

THE seventh and last petition of the Lord's Prayer. That it is indeed a seventh petition, and not to be counted (with some divines) as part of the sixth, is evident. The subject-matter of the first is Temptation. The subject-matter of the second is Evil. Now temptation and evil are not identical, nor even coextensive; they do not cover the same field. As Bishop Andrewes pithily observes: 'Every evil is not temptation, neither is every temptation evil.' Sin is the evil of evils, the greatest and most fundamental evil. But sin and temptation are by no means identical, though they are often confounded. To be severely tempted is not necessarily to sin. Our Lord, we are told, 'was tempted in all points like as we are, yet without sin' either in act or tendency.

Yet while we stoutly maintain such a distinctness of idea in these two clauses as constitutes them separate petitions, we would at the same time recognize their intimately close connexion, which is indicated by the conjunction 'but.'

In reciting the paraphrase, which is given in the Catechism of this part of the Prayer, children often make a mistake, the correction of which may be profitable to older persons, and give some insight into the connexion we are in search of. Instead of saying, 'That it will please Him to save and defend us *in* all dangers, ghostly and bodily,' they alter the preposition, and say, '*From* all dangers, ghostly and bodily.' This gives the teacher the opportunity of explaining that to be saved *in* danger is a very different thing from being saved *from* danger. He who never crosses the water is saved, by this precaution, *from* the dangers of the sea; but he who puts out to sea amidst shoals, and rocks, and quicksands, and is brought safely through all to the end of his voyage, is saved *in* the dangers of the sea. One escapes by not running the risk, the other escapes in running it. Now in spiritual matters it is our heavenly Father's will that we should all of us undergo risks in one form or another. None of us can be allowed to stay at home; we must all put out to sea. Is it not life appointed for probation of a Christian? Is it not God's object, in leading us through the wilderness of the world, 'to prove' us, 'that He may know what is in' our 'hearts'? No circumstances can ever be, none ever are, exempt from temptation; for where there is exemption from temptation there can be no room for probation. You may try to discover a shady nook in life, secluded from public notice, and from the snares which beset those who live in the great world; but the nook is no harbour of refuge; it has its perils as well as the open sea. You cannot shut the door upon the devil. The devil is busy in churches as well as in theatres; in what is called religious, as well as in what is called worldly, society; in an atmosphere of piety as well as in an atmosphere where everything is avowedly regulated by this world's maxims. Give yourself to literary seclusion, and you are apt to fall into the snare of intellectual pride. Give yourself to religious seclusion, so that life shall be one ceaseless round of prayer and meditation, and you no less certainly incur the danger of spiritual pride. Embark on a sacred pursuit with the idea that it will shield you, and you will soon experience the fearful aptness of familiarity with holy things to deaden our reverence for them, and to turn the edge of religious impressions. If God gives you the happy competency which is so much longed for and so loudly praised, great is the risk which He gives you with it of settling down into a lukewarm life, stirred by no breath of spiritual aspiration, a life in which the moral element is hardly at all a feature. If He trusts you only with one talent, there arises immediately a temptation to say, 'Is it not a little one?' and on that ground to cover it up in a napkin, and to hide it away in the earth. If He surrounds you with the domestic affections, and gives you a quiet and a happy home, you may easily fall into the snare of loving father

But Deliver us from Evil

or mother, son or daughter, wife or child more than Him, and so in the end may prove unworthy of Him. Great are the temptations to impurity in celibacy. Great are the temptations to worldly carefulness in marriage. A life of leisure is full of temptations to indolence; a life of business, full of temptations to neglect prayer and to ignore claims upon our sympathy. If you live too much alone, you shall become selfish; if too much in company, you shall be entangled and hampered by secular ties. Change in position, age, circumstances will bring no real relief; it will eventually prove nothing more than the exchange of one class of trials for another. This universal prevalence of temptation in all positions is probably indicated in that obscure title which is given to the tempter in the Epistle to the Ephesians, 'the prince of the power of the air.' The air is everywhere; or rather in every place which men can reach to, and where they can exist. A supply of air is a condition of natural life, and natural life would collapse without it. Similarly temptation, of which Satan was the first originator, and with which he has still so much to do, is a condition of moral life. It travels with us wherever we go; we inhale it as the element in which we live, and move; we can no more avoid it than a bird, by taking wing, can avoid the atmosphere. He may soar to the highest pinnacle of the Temple, or creep into an obscure cranny in the heart of a decayed oak; but alike in both positions he finds the atmosphere there before him.

God then saves us IN, and not FROM, spiritual dangers, although we may lawfully pray to be altogether shielded from such dangers as would overwhelm our courage, overtax our strength, and lay prostrate our faith. And the 'but' at the beginning of this petition tacitly recognizes temptation as a Divine ordinance for man. The two petitions with their connective particle may be paraphrased thus: 'Place me not by Thy providence in situations of trial, nor suffer the devil to try me above my strength, nor withdraw Thy Spirit from me when I am tempted; *but* since temptation is Thine uniform appointment and our inevitable lot, in all those temptations, which it is Thy will that I should endure, deliver me from the evil to which the temptation might lead, so that I may not receive any detriment thereby.' It is exactly the line of thought, in which the mind of our blessed Lord travels when He says, in interceding for His disciples, 'I pray not that Thou shouldst take them out of the world; but that thou shouldest keep them from the evil.' To take them out of the world would conflict with Thy design and appointment for them; they are to be 'the salt of the earth and the light of the world,' and must therefore come in contact with that society which they are to be the means of enlightening and preserving from corruption; but from the taint of worldly sentiments and worldly ways, and so eventually from the awful doom of being 'conformed to and condemned with the world,' I pray that they may be delivered by Thy grace.

What then is 'the' evil, from which we sue to be delivered in this petition? The word employed in the original, according to its etymology, means that which causes toil or hardship, and so does injury or mischief; and it might with great force be rendered in the passage before us, 'Deliver us from that which is mischievous,' this being as nearly as possible equivalent to the petition in one of our collects, 'We humbly beseech Thee to put away from us all hurtful things.'

Now it must stand to reason that, in teaching us to pray against that which does mischief, our Lord must intend to fix our thoughts principally, though not exclusively, upon the source of all mischief. And this source of all mischief is sin. Sin is mischievous, not only to the bodies of men which shall die, and to the circumstances of men which shall pass away, but to their souls, i.e. to their characters, which shall endure in another condition of existence. The ancients had a fable of Pandora, that she was a woman framed by the gods to bring misery upon the human race, and wonderfully endowed for that purpose. A box was given her by the gods, in which they had enclosed all kinds of evils and troubles, and at the bottom, hope. She persuaded Epimetheus to open the box, so that all the evils and troubles escaped, and spread over the earth. With difficulty the box was closed again in time to preserve hope, the last and lowest of its contents [1]. Probably this is the fabulous, legendary form, which the true history of our first mother's act took among the old heathens. Her act of eating the forbidden fruit—an act stimulated, it would appear, by a desire of larger knowledge than her Maker saw fit to communicate—an act of pure sin, as distinct from an act of immorality, that is, a simple violation of the will of God, as expressed in a restriction arbitrarily imposed—this act set open the floodgates of misery and inundated the world with evil. Yet still our Pandora and her colleague contrived to detain or imprison hope, in virtue not of her own deserts, but of God's most gracious and comfortable promise. The woman had brought the mischief; but the woman was to bring also, in some mysterious manner, the seed who should repair the mischief, and who is expressly called by St. Paul 'the Lord Jesus Christ who is our

[1] Bacon's *Wisdom of the Ancients*, No. 26.

hope.' And it is in hope of God's mercy through Christ, and of Christ's grace, being extended to us, that we now pray: 'Deliver us from evil—from the mischief which has gone forth over the face of the whole earth, and is now everywhere abroad.'

Yet while it is maintained that sin is the evil of evils, the most fundamental and the most formidable of all evils, so that in comparison with the least departure from God's will, bodily pain, disease, pestilence, famine, earthquake, flood, and fire are altogether light calamities; while it is maintained that 'the sting' of all natural evil, and 'of death,' the greatest natural evil, is 'sin,' and that where sin has loosed its hold upon the heart of man, these evils have lost their sting; we may not put so unnatural a strain upon this truth as to deny the existence of evil in disease or other forms of natural calamity. Our blessed Lord did not teach stoicism respecting outward disasters; on the other hand He inculcated the simple and natural view of them, and manifested for those who suffered for them an unbounded sympathy.

When applied to for cures, He universally bestowed them; and in several cases, attracted by His own divine compassion, He called to the sufferer, addressed to him or her a few words, to revive the dying embers of hope in his heart, and then restored him by an act of miraculous power. The main object of His coming was no doubt to break the power of sin over the human heart. But He did not as a fact break this spiritual power of sin, without concurrently breaking in a thousand instances its natural power: 'Whithersoever He entered, into villages, or cities, or country, they laid the sick in the streets, and besought Him that they might touch if it were but the border of His garment: and as many as touched Him were made whole.'

We find our warrant then for prayers against all forms of natural evil in this last petition of the Lord's Prayer: 'Deliver us from that which is mischievous'—in other words, 'Put away from us all hurtful things'; 'Save and defend us in all dangers, not ghostly only, but bodily also'; 'From lightning and tempest; from plague, pestilence, and famine; from battle and murder, and from sudden death, Good Lord, deliver us.'

But attention should be pointedly called to the fact that this petition is the last in the Lord's Prayer, and presupposes that the heart and soul of the petitioner has gone along with the previous petitions. It is to be taken in connexion with all that has preceded, and postponed to them all.

Men who care little for the honour of God, or even for spiritual blessings to themselves, are ready enough to cry to Him for deliverance from the evils of human life when the thundercloud of adversity blackens and breaks over their heads.

Nor does our most merciful Father then turn a deaf ear to His children, except under special circumstances.

But this is but the maimed trunk of the childlike prayer taught by the Lord. The habitually prayerful Christian places *foremost* God's fatherly character, His honour, kingdom, and will, and only at last reaches the idea of man's deliverance from some pressing emergency.

But there is another significance in the final position of this petition. It leaves us not saddened with the thought of evil. It opens a vista of the glorious future of the Christian Church. For the prayer, 'Deliver us from evil,' will never be fully and completely answered until a condition of existence supervenes, of which we have no present experience. Neither sin, nor the consequences of sin, will entirely lose their hold upon us, and let us go free, until those times of the restitution of all things, which shall be ushered in by the second advent of Christ.

So long as death, and the various agencies which contribute to death, linger here below, the Church of God cannot be fully delivered from evil. Potentially indeed evil has been extirpated by the work of Christ; or, in other words, His person and work are powers introduced into the moral system of man, which are sufficient ultimately to secure a triumph over all evil; but the experience of every day teaches forcibly that evil is not yet actually abolished. Nor, whatever Utopian dreams some may entertain of the prospects of our race, and whatever vaunts others may make of the actual progress of man, can evil ever be abolished by any other agency than that of a second manifestation of the Saviour.

There is loud boasting of the advance of physical and linguistic science, of the enormous spread of secular education among the working classes, as 'ameliorating' (in the cant of the day) the condition of humanity. But it is more than doubtful whether there is any increase of faith in God, any diminution of rebellion against Him, even in Christian nations. The great exhibitions of national industry which we have witnessed in our times, the march of intellect and the progress of Europe in the arts of peace which we hear so loudly applauded, have evidently done nothing whatever to extirpate from the hearts of kings and statesmen that greed of territory, that lust of dominion, which are the origin of sanguinary wars; and a devil perhaps might smile sardonically, as an angel might be conceived to weep, on remarking that the chief bearing of what is called human progress on these wars is the invention of weapons which mow down soldiers by scores, where our ancestors used to kill them in detail by units. And as for death, has science or the progress of civilization at all materially affected its prevalence? What if the modern physician can add a few more years to his patient's span, or alleviate his pain somewhat more effectually than with his few herbs and simples the ancient one could? It is no great triumph after all, when it is considered that the creature thus temporarily relieved must exist for ever. If the threescore years and ten now be prolonged to fourscore, the fourscore must come to an end, a little later. A man's house may be furnished with all that can make this life agreeable and refined; but he cannot live in it for ever. He must be carried out one day, and laid in the sepulchre. And when that time comes, his few more years, or the alleviations of his condition at the close of life, will seem to him a very small matter, in view of the new and untried experiences on which he is entering.

But assuredly, as God is true, all the deliverance for which man yearns—deliverance from evil, moral, natural, social—awaits His redeemed in future. The Deliverer, when He comes the second time, shall bring it with Him. The hopes of our race are wrapped up in His Divine person, and can only be fulfilled by His own personal agency. Therefore we, who are tossed in the vessel of His Church on the waves of this troublesome world, look for His glorious appearing in this final petition of our Prayer. Like the crew in St. Paul's ship, we cast four anchors out of the stern—the anchors of faith, hope, love, and allegiance to present duty—and wait for the day. Glorious beyond anything which natural sunrise can shadow forth will be the morning of the advent and the resurrection of the saints.

For the Son of Righteousness will rise, with healing in His wings for every malady of His people; and the dead in Christ will bestir themselves to meet Him, and will recognize joyfully Him whom, having not seen, they have so long and so dearly loved; and all shadows which have rested upon the truth and providence of God, as well as those which have darkened man's estate, shall flee away; and the perfect coming of the kingdom shall be also a perfect deliverance from evil; for 'there shall be no more death, neither sorrow nor crying, neither shall there be any more pain' (Rev. xxi. 4).

CHAPTER XVI

FOR THINE IS THE KINGDOM, AND THE POWER, AND THE GLORY, FOR EVER.—AMEN

IN the second section of the Lord's Prayer we have turned our thoughts to the condition of man here below; to his wants, his sins, his temptations, his dangers. We have used a familiar language in so doing; we have spoken with 'the tongues of men'; for on all sides the accents of human distress and human trial (natural or spiritual) break upon our ear. But in passing on to the Doxology[1] we change our language and speak with 'the tongues of angels.'

---

[1] The Dean does not discuss the doubts cast upon the text of the Doxology by most modern editors of St. Matthew's Gospel; as he did not discuss the question of the independent records of the Lord's Prayer, p. 62 note.

It is omitted in the three most ancient MSS. which still exist of this part of the New Testament. It is however

For Thine is the Kingdom

We join ourselves to the heavenly hierarchy, and recite the anthem of praise, which they also recite in a realm where want, sin, and trial are unknown.

Moreover praise is the legitimate and ordained issue of prayer. If the heart is filled with God's blessings drawn down into it by prayer, it will expand towards God in praise. The Psalter, found in a large number of later MSS., some of which may possibly represent copies still older than those which have recently been assumed to be almost exclusive authorities for the text of the New Testament. Most of the versions, and all the earlier Greek commentators from Origen downwards (except St. Chrysostom and his personal followers), support it. Moreover, its liturgical use, though a plausible account of a possible introduction into the Scripture, does not negative its previous existence in the Scripture.

Whether or not it formed part of the Lord's Sermon on the Mount was therefore not unanimously determined by the ancients, and cannot now be positively settled by the moderns.

But even if it has not our Lord's personal authority, 'it was added,' says a venerable writer of the fifth century, 'by the divine luminaries and masters of the Church as the concluding acclamation of the Prayer.'

At least, therefore, the Doxology has on it so high a stamp of Church authority that it must be accepted as sanctioned by the Holy Ghost to be the Church's refrain of our Lord's own sentiments, the octave of His keynote of human prayer.— B. C.

viewed as a consecutive book of devotions, illustrates this, the earliest Psalms being for the most part supplicatory, sometimes even plaintive, but the whole collection ending with noblest bursts of praise, the close of all being, 'Let everything that hath breath' (breath by the cunning device of man, like a wind instrument, and breath by the nobler inspiration of God, the living voice of man and animals) 'praise the Lord.'

Indeed it would seem that this Doxology may have been drawn from the recorded words of David himself. For thus did that devout king, after making large preparations for the building of the temple by his successor, bless the Lord: 'Thine, O Lord, is the greatness, and the *power*, and the *glory*, and the victory, and the majesty; for all that is in the heaven and in the earth is Thine; Thine is the *kingdom*, O Lord, and Thou art exalted as head above all.' You will observe that in the ascription of praise now before us *three* attributes are selected out of a larger number specified by David—'the kingdom, and the power, and the glory,' a beautiful glimpse being thus opened, at the close of the prayer, of the mystery of the great Triune Name into which, before His ascension, our Lord bade His apostles baptize their converts, thereby formally making disciples. Observe that the unity of the Godhead comes out at the opening of the prayer, the address being made to the Father, as the fountain of Deity. And then, like some beautiful flower which, so long as it is in the bud or only half-opened, is not seen to present distinction of parts, but when it has fully expanded, under the influence of dew and sunshine, shows three stamens rising up from the calix, this address to the heavenly Father, when it has reached its full blossom, insinuates the distinction of three several Persons in the bosom of the Godhead, inasmuch as 'the *kingdom*' of God, which now is, as distinct from that which is to be, is the mediatorial kingdom of *the Son*; and *the power* by which that kingdom is being advanced is the power of *the Holy Ghost*; and *the glory* of founding, furthering, and consummating this kingdom will be poured ultimately into the treasury of *the Father*.

'Thine,' we say first, 'is the kingdom.' Now

observe that when we previously spoke of the kingdom it was in the terms of a holy wish or devout inspiration, not of an affirmation. We said, 'Thy kingdom' (i. e. our Father's kingdom) 'come.' We now assert that God's kingdom exists already; 'Thine is the kingdom.' The apparent inconsistency is soon explained by a reference to Holy Scripture. The apostle St. Paul teaches us that God the Father is at present governing the Church and the world, not immediately, but by a representative and vicegerent, the Lord Jesus Christ, God manifest in the flesh; and that this administration of Jesus Christ in the place of God the Father (typified by Joseph's administration in Egypt in the place of Pharaoh) has an appointed term, which is thus described: 'Then cometh the end, when He shall have delivered up the kingdom to God, even the Father; when He shall have put down all rule and all authority and power. For He must reign, till He hath put all enemies under His feet. The last enemy that shall be destroyed is death. For He hath put all things under His feet. But when he saith all things are put under Him, it is manifest that He is excepted, which did put all things under Him. And when all things shall be subdued unto Him, then shall the Son also Himself be subject unto Him that put all things under Him, that God may be all in all' (1 Cor. xv. 24-28). Now in the petition, 'Thy kingdom come,' it is rather the final and more immediate kingdom of God the Father, as lying in the future, which we have in view; whereas in this ascription, 'Thine is the kingdom,' our thoughts are rather fastened upon the mediatorial kingdom, under which we now exist, and which indeed constitutes the present economy.

But is Christ indeed reigning? some may ask. What evidence do the things which are seen furnish of the present existence of His kingdom? Beyond the two Sacraments of the Gospel and other rites of our religion which are administered among us, little enough. Nineteen centuries have dragged their slow length along, since He returned to the heaven from which He was sent forth. During that long lapse of time every kind of heresy and contradiction has shot up in the society which He founded; there is scarcely any form of misbelief, or of unbelief, or of sin, which the Church has not witnessed, nay, which has not been developed in her bosom Even the wiser part of those who should watch for the bridegroom have slumbered and slept. Under these painful circumstances, is Christ really governing? or have the reins of administration slipped from His hands? It is quite clear that unless we firmly believe Him to be governing, despite all appearances to the contrary, we cannot say sincerely, 'Thine is the kingdom.' But it is the province of faith to make this glorious affirmation, appearances notwithstanding.

Faith calls to mind the word of prophecy. She remembers that not a bright, but a very dark, future was predicted for the Church. The Church was to be a field overrun with tares; a draw-net, which gathered fish of every kind, good and bad. 'The Spirit spake expressly, that in the latter times some should depart from the faith, giving heed to seducing spirits, and doctrines of devils; speaking lies in hypocrisy;

having their conscience seared with a hot iron' (1 Tim. iv. 1, 2).

Antichrists were many in the days of the apostle St. John; and were at length to culminate and grow to a frightful head in one great antichrist, an awful person, to be revealed in the latter days. The first ministers of the new dispensation expressly say that agencies antagonistic to the mediatorial kingdom—counterworking it, so far as it is permitted to the creature to counterwork the Creator—abounded in their times. 'Now we see not yet all things put under Him.' So that faith's assurance that Christ is at present administering the kingdom is not seriously chilled by noticing the outward prevalence of unbelief, sin, and all the ills which flesh is heir to. 'These things,' says faith, 'were all foreseen, predicted, provided for. If there were no evil counteracting the Saviour, there would be no evidence of the surpassing skill and wisdom, or of the extraordinary patience and longsuffering, with which He administers the affairs of the kingdom. To see Him presiding at the helm of His Church in a calm, when the sun shines and wind and tide favour the ship's progress, and she speeds on the wings of an auspicious breeze towards the haven of glory, would furnish no proof of His skill or power as a pilot. But let the vessel of the Church labour in the storm heavily; let her be tossed with waves, so that the ship is wellnigh full; let her be in danger ever and anon of foundering, and then let Him arouse Himself from sleep and with a word extricate her from her grievous peril, and enrich her, by means of her past trials, with many precious lessons of experience, and give her a larger reach of faith and a stronger yearning of hope, and then shall we indeed know that "the Lord reigneth"; that His divine wisdom and love are employed in His administration; that "His is the kingdom," and that He is ordering to God's glory and to the welfare of His own people even "the unruly wills and affections of sinful men."'

The next thing which we profess in this ascription is that 'God's is the power'; the power, that is, which is gradually establishing and will eventually consummate the kingdom. The word used in the original is that which is appropriated in the New Testament to the expression of moral and spiritual, as distinct from physical, force. And standing in this connexion, it shows the nature of the kingdom. It implies, what is elsewhere expressly asserted, that it is internal and spiritual, and furthered by internal and spiritual agencies. 'The kingdom of God cometh not with observation; neither shall they say, Lo here! or, lo there! for, behold, the kingdom of God is within you' (St. Luke xvii. 20, 21). This being the case, it is no wonder if the things which are seen give but little notice of the existence or progress of the kingdom. It is an object of faith, and not of sight. If it pleased God to lay open to us what He carefully conceals, the whole theatre of the moral world—the hearts and characters of all men, and the various agencies which from different quarters are being brought to bear on those hearts and characters—we should then no more doubt of the existence and development of Christ's spiritual kingdom than we can question the existence and the wide spread of the

English empire. And observe whose is this spiritual force which is abroad in the world, and which, marching hand in hand with Divine Providence, is gradually bringing all things into subjection to Christ, and putting all things under His feet. It is the power of God the Holy Ghost. 'My speech and my preaching,' says St. Paul, 'was not with enticing words of man's wisdom, but in demonstration of *the Spirit* and of *power.*' And again: 'Our Gospel came not unto you in word only, but also in power, and in the Holy Ghost, and in much assurance' (1 Thess. i. 5).

The third profession which we make in this ascription is that 'to God belongs the glory.' The word 'glory' is often used with the vaguest possible notion of its import. The Greek word which is so translated is etymologically connected with a verb meaning 'to esteem,' or 'account.' The substantive therefore means originally 'estimation,' 'reputation'—the credit which a person gains, the esteem in which he is held for any excellence which he possesses, or any exploit he performs. We shall take the word here in this its earliest sense; and regard

God's 'glory' as meaning the credit of His character, the estimation in which He is held among His rational creatures. And the assertion is that to God supremely—to 'the God and Father of our Lord Jesus Christ'—belongs the credit of establishing the kingdom of Christ by the power of the Holy Ghost, and the credit of every blessing, spiritual and temporal, which is conferred on the subjects of that kingdom. The counsel of redemption originated with the Father, for 'God so loved the world that He gave His only-begotten Son' out of His bosom, to save sinners; it has been furthered in every step by Him who also 'sent forth the Spirit of His Son into your hearts, crying, Abba, Father' (Gal. iv. 6); and as each soul is delivered from the burden of the flesh, and gathered safely under the Redeemer's wing, the holy angels ascribe to God all the glory of its salvation. And when all things have been put under the Redeemer's feet, when sin is extirpated and death abolished, and, the purposes for which it exists having been fully answered, the mediatorial kingdom is laid down, when the Son Himself becomes subject unto Him that put all things under Him, and God is all in all, then shall the ascription, 'Thine is the glory' receive its fullest verification, and the praise of the Father shall thrill, with one strong pulsation, through the rational universe. To the very furthest point, then, in the horizon of the future does this ascription stretch forward. And the devout Christian makes it, not in a spirit of faith only, rising above present appearances and his immediate surroundings, but in a spirit of hope also, looking for and hasting unto the day when evil shall be finally abolished, and when in the hearts of His saved and glorified people there shall be no note which is not perfectly attuned to our heavenly Father's praise.

But what is the connexion of this Doxology with the body of the Prayer? what the exact significance of the conjunction 'for,' which is the link of connexion?

'For,' then, expresses our ground of confidence that the petitions which we have offered will receive an answer. Because God has the supreme authority, and all power necessary to give effect to His authority, and because every blessing which He confers will redound to His glory, therefore we believe that He will hear us, who are the subjects of His Son's kingdom.

And the recital of these our grounds of confidence, while it is an encouragement to ourselves, is also an argument to induce God to hear us.

First, it is an encouragement to ourselves. We have arrived at the end of our prayer—a period when the hands are apt to hang down and the knees to become feeble. We have asked much. We have travelled far in the path of spiritual desire. But we must not faint, if we desire to carry away the blessing. The hands of Moses, as he interceded on the Mount, grew heavy with weariness; but, as victory over Amalek was dependent upon their continual uplifting, means were resorted to for holding them up. So, before we close our Prayer, we make an effort to lift up the drooping hands by glancing at the sovereign authority, universal control, and illustrious renown of our God; by reminding ourselves that His is the kingdom, and the power, and the glory.

But by reciting our grounds of confidence

we not only encourage ourselves, but move God to give ear to our cry. When we say, '*Thine* is the kingdom, and the power, and the glory,' we remind God that it is His matter, and not ours only, which we bring before Him; that His glory is concerned in helping and relieving us. In short, the last petition and the Doxology of the Lord's Prayer find their paraphrase in those supplications of the Litany: 'O Lord, arise, help us, and deliver us for Thy Name's sake—for Thine honour.'

This seeking to interest God in ourselves by considerations drawn from His own glory has its warrant in numberless passages of Holy Scripture—such, for example, as this from the prophet Ezekiel: 'Thus saith the Lord God; I do not this for your sakes, O house of Israel, but for Mine holy name's sake' (Ezek. xxxvi. 22); and this from the Psalms: 'They provoked Him at the sea, even at the Red sea. Nevertheless He saved them for His name's sake, that He might make His mighty power to be known.' God's supreme motive in all things that He does is revealed as His own glory—a position sound and scriptural in itself, though sometimes most unscripturally misrepresented and misunderstood. When it is said that God seeks in all things His own glory, this must be taken in connexion with the other statement that 'God is love.' God is not a self-seeking being (forbid it, Lord, that we should ever so horribly misconceive of Thee); the glory which He seeks is the glory of pure, intense, ardent love. And love is so far from self-seeking that it is self-sacrificing; or in other words, the attribute of love is the very contradictory of self-seeking. 'God so loved the world that He gave,' out of His bosom, 'His only-begotten Son' (St. John iii. 16). Christ so loved men that He laid down His life for them. And thus, when it is said that His own glory is God's great motive, what is meant is that He seeks in all things to glorify love and truth, which are the essential constituents of the Divine character. And so, when we say to Him, 'Thine is the glory,' we humbly suggest that, by helping us, He will be furthering the cause of love and truth, which is in fact His own cause.

Amen sums up all that precedes. It is transliterated, not translated, from the Hebrew, transplanted from the use of the Synagogue to that of the Christian Church. St. Cyril of Jerusalem, in commenting upon the Lord's Prayer, as it stood in the canon of the Liturgy, and was recited in connexion with the prayer of Consecration, says that we set our seal upon the Lord's Prayer when we respond to it by a fervent Amen. This expression may perhaps give us a wider insight into the force and significance of Amen than we have hitherto gained. Our Catechism Englishes it, we all know, by 'so be it'—a rendering which recognizes no more in Amen than the expression of Christian desire. And, as it stands at the end of prayers, this is no doubt part of its meaning, though by no means the whole. In order fully to seize its significance it should be borne in mind that the original word is an adjective, signifying 'firm' or 'faithful,' and, when used adverbially, 'truly, surely, verily.' If a verb has to be supplied there is nothing in the word Amen to indicate what its mood and tense shall be, which therefore must be determined by the context. When a desire is expressed in the context, as it is in every petition, the Amen signifies that the person who says it assents to the desire. When merely an affirmation is made, as in the sentences of God's wrath in the Commination Service, and as in our Lord's words at the end of St. Matthew's Gospel, 'Lo, I am with you even unto the end of the world, Amen,' the Amen signifies that the person who says it either assents to the affirmation if another has made it, or confirms it if he has made it himself. When the Lord's Prayer is succeeded by the Doxology, the word must evidently express assent both to the petitions of the Prayer, and to the affirmations of the Doxology (the Doxology of course being an affirmation and not strictly a prayer). But even in prayers which are merely petitions, and which are not succeeded by an ascription of praise to God, we desire to vindicate for Amen the meaning of 'so it is' as well as of 'so be it.' It is something more than the voice of desire; it is the voice of faith also. It is the setting of our seal upon the prayer, says St. Cyril, this expression connecting itself easily and naturally with St. John the Baptist's words, 'He that hath received' Christ's 'testimony hath set to his seal'—put his seal to the assertion—'that God is true' (St. John iii. 33). He who says Amen to a prayer not only expresses a wish that God may give, but also a belief that He does and will give (in His own good time and way). And since the petitions of the Lord's Prayer, being put into our mouth by the Lord Himself, cannot but be for things expedient, we may confidently believe—nay we ought to believe—that God gives them to us; and the Amen with which we close the prayer should mean, in a large paraphrase, just this: 'This is the confidence that we have in Him, that if we ask anything according to His will, He heareth us'; and, as what our Lord teaches us to ask must be 'according to His will,' we know that when we offer them fervently and humbly 'we have the petitions that we desired of him' (1 John v. 15). Let our Amen be thus the voice of faith, and our recitation of the Divine prayer shall not be without large success.

For He hath said, 'What things soever ye desire when ye pray, believe that ye have received[1] them, and ye shall have them' (St. Mark xi. 24).

In conclusion; let us fail not to observe how, in the ascription, the Prayer which in its earliest section was occupied with God, with His honour, kingdom, and will, closes upon the same key in which it opened. The 'us' and 'our' of the second section flow back again into the 'Thine' of the first. Like a river which, taking its rise in the fountains of the great deep, loses itself again, after it has run its course, in the reservoir of the sea; so the Lord's Prayer, which took its rise in the thought of God, and commenced with expressions of devotion and affiance, ends with similar thoughts and similar expressions. The mental eye is not suffered to rest on our wants, sins, trials, nor on self in any shape, lest it should become jaundiced. It is purged at the beginning, purged again at the end, by being made to gaze on the love and the loftiness, on the power and glory of our God. Alas! how our best and most earnest prayers come

---

[1] The tense of this verb is past, not future.—B. C.

short when judged by such a standard! How often has prayer sunk down with us into a mere whining recital of our needs, in which there has been no thought of the beauty and blessedness of the Divine character, nor indeed any loftier desire than that of relief under an immediate pressure! Let us learn in deepest humility to look God more in the face when we pray, to set His revealed character more steadily before the eyes of our mind. Let us occupy our hearts with His perfections, and He will occupy Himself with our wants. The real balm for the troubled spirit is to be sought in the consideration of His fatherhood, His sovereignty, His controlling wisdom, His irresistible power, His boundless love. Think more of these, and less of our own distresses, and the balm shall begin to distill; even 'The peace of God, which passeth all understanding, and shall keep our hearts and minds through Christ Jesus.'

www.ingramcontent.com/pod-product-compliance
Lightning Source LLC
Chambersburg PA
CBHW030747250426
43672CB00028B/1225